The Christian Doctrine of Sin
By John Tulloch, D.D.
Edited by AnthonyUyl

Woodstock, Ontario, 2016

The Christian Doctrine of Sin
By John Tulloch, D.D.
Principal of St. Mary's College in the University of St. Andrew's; One of Her Majesty's Chaplains For Scotland

Edited by Anthony Uyl

Originally Published by:
New York; Scribner, Armstrong & Co.; Grant, Faires & Rodgers, Electrotypers and Printers, 52 & 54 N. Sixth St., Philadelphia

The text of The Christian Doctrine of Sin is all in the Public Domain. This edition is published by Devoted Publishing a division of 2165467 Ontario Inc.

What kind of philosophies do you have?
Let us know!

Contact us at: devotedpub@hotmail.com
Visit us on Facebook: Devoted Publishing
Get more products via our website: www.devotedpublishing.com
Published in Woodstock, Ontario, Canada 2016.

For bulk educational rates, please contact us as the above email address.

ISBN: 978-1-988297-18-7

John Tulloch, D.D.

Table of Contents

PREFATORY NOTE 4
I - THE QUESTION OF SIN IN RELATION TO MODERN SCHOOLS OF THOUGHT - METHOD OF TREATMENT 5
II - IDEA OF EVIL OUTSIDE OF REVELATION 12
III - OLD TESTAMENT DOCTRINE OF SIN 20
IV - DOCTRINE OF SIN AS CONTAINED IN THE GOSPELS 30
V - DOCTRINE OF ST. PAUL'S EPISTLES 40
VI - ORIGINAL SIN 49
APPENDIX 57
    I 57
    II 57
    III 58
    IV 60
    V 61
    VI 62
    VII 62
    VIII 63
    IX 63
    X 63
    XI 64
    XII 64
    XIII 65
    XIV 65
    XV 66
    XVI 67
    XVII 67
    XVIII 67
    XIX 68
    XX 68
    XXI 69

PREFATORY NOTE

I HAD intended to enlarge this volume so as to embrace a special discussion of the Augustinian and subsequent developments of the Doctrine of Sin in the thought of the Church. I wished also to treat of the bearing on this doctrine of certain modern theories, from the Optimism of Leibnitz to the Pessimism of Schopenhauer and Hartmann. But the consideration of these later aspects of the subject must be deferred. It was deemed desirable that the present Lectures should appear without delay, and as much as possible in the form in which they were delivered. The volume answers to its title with sufficient distinctness; and although nothing new can be said on such a subject, the method of treatment may be found to have for readers something of the same interest that it had for the numerous hearers who attended the delivery of the Lectures.

June 1, 1876.

John Tulloch, D.D.

I – THE QUESTION OF SIN IN RELATION TO MODERN SCHOOLS OF THOUGHT – METHOD OF TREATMENT

THE subject which I have undertaken to discuss in these Lectures, if it cannot be said to lie at the foundation of Christian Theology, is more or less implied in the whole system of Christian doctrine. In itself it belongs to what in modern nomenclature is called Anthropology rather than Theology. It is a question, that is to say, respecting Man rather than God. But the Christian conception of God, and of God's action in the world, points throughout to man as a sinner. All the characteristic terms of Christian Theology--salvation, redemption, forgiveness, grace--indicate that there is a power of evil from which man needs to be saved, or which impedes his higher life. There can be no more important inquiry, therefore, than one into the reality and the meaning of this power of evil, which Christians call sin.

It is interesting to trace, both in Theology and Philosophy, the interdependence of what may be called Anthropological and Theological questions. Man's conception of himself, of his own nature, is never separable from his higher conception of the Divine. He is really, even when his thoughts seem to wander furthest away or most aloft, the pivot round which they turn. What he is himself, or is supposed to be, gives the colour to all he thinks of Nature around him, and God above him. There never was a vainer effort than that so much vaunted at present of casting aside anthropological ideas. No more than man can strip himself of his nature can he strip his thought of the folds in which that nature enwraps it. There is a sense, and a right sense, in which man's thought of himself--what he is--must mould all his other thought, philosophical as well as theological.

In the history of the Church this has been exemplified over and over again. A shallow conception of man's nature has always bred a shallow conception of the Divine nature. A meagre anthropology has for its counterpart a meagre theology. A Pelagian not merely denies the depth of human sin, but the profundities of the Divine action. And the same law of alternation or balance, if not always in the same marked degree, runs everywhere through the long line of the development of Christian thought.

But the antithesis is not less marked in Philosophy. From the earliest dawn of speculation two sides everywhere appear, contrasted by their starting-point not less than by their results. It is the conception of man as a being not only mundane, but supra-mundane--as drawing his higher life from a higher source--which has alone given rise to a higher philosophy, or a Philosophy of Being. The conception of man as merely a consensus of external faculties has never risen above a philosophy of the senses. Nor could it be otherwise. Thought cannot, any more than water, rise higher than its source. And the thought that is solely earth-born, or the inheritance of mundane experiences, and nothing more--however subtilised or aspiring--can never bring any light from beyond its earthly home. We must start from a higher home, from a "heaven lying about us in our infancy," if we would ever reach a spiritual and higher line of thought at all. We cannot climb into an empty heaven. If we are not born with the "promise and potency" of the Divine, the "image of God," within us, then we shall never reach the Divine, earnestly as we may grope for it, and cast forth our loftiest thoughts to grasp it.

The present turn of speculation once more strikingly illustrates this interdependence of thought on these great subjects. The favourite conceptions of modern science involve, if they do not start from, a definite view of human nature at variance with the old Biblical or spiritual view. Man is conceived as developed from lower forms of life by lengthened processes of natural selection. There is nothing necessarily inconsistent with an enlightened Christianity in this idea, so far. The Divine mind may work out its plans by processes of growth or adaptation as readily as by any other way. Nay, as it has been recently admitted by one of the most distinguished advocates of the modern idea, the teleological conception, or the conception of design, is prominently suggested rather than excluded by the theory of development as a mere modus operandi. But beyond question the chief advocates of this theory mean something very different. Nature is supposed by them to be not merely the sphere of operation, but the operating power itself--beyond which there is nothing. Man is not merely, like all other things, a natural growth, but he is nothing else. There is no higher Divine element in him. There is no such thing--or at least nothing that we can know or validly infer. Material facts and their relations or laws are all that we can ever know. It is this underlying sense of the theory which is at variance with the old Biblical view of human nature. It leaves, for example, no room for the idea of sin. For that which is solely a growth of nature cannot contain anything that is at variance with its own higher laws. It may show more or less perfect stages of growth, but it cannot contradict itself. If the individual and social man alike are merely the outcome of natural forces working endlessly forward towards higher and more complex forms, then whatever man is, he is not and cannot be a sinner. The mixed product of internal and external forces--of what is called organism and environment--he may be at certain stages of his progress very defective. It may require thousands of years to elevate him into a more complete existence. But he has not fallen below any ideal he might have reached. He has not wilfully rejected a good he might have known. He is only at any point what the sum of natural factors which enter into his being have made him. The two conceptions of sin and of development in this naturalistic sense cannot coexist. I cannot be the mere outcome of natural law, and yet accountable for the fact that I am no better than I am. If I am only the child of nature, I must be entitled to the privileges of nature. If I have come from matter alone, then, I cannot dwell within the shadow of a responsibility whose birthplace is elsewhere--in a different region altogether. And so the spirit of modern science is consistently non-Christian. A man who is nothing more than an aggregate of natural powers, can have no true vision transcending the range of these powers. The Unseen, or a law coming forth from the Unseen to rule his spirit, must be a mere superstition to him, and sin, as the violation of such a law, a mere gloomy phantom, to be got rid of the best way he can.

These considerations may serve to show the importance of our subject, and how vitally it bears on the problems of modern thought. All these problems, and indeed the problems of thought in all ages, have circulated around two main modes of conceiving human nature--the one of which is spiritual, Biblical, and theistic, and the other natural, cosmical, and anti-theistic. These are the real antitheses which underlie all human speculation, and to which it always returns. It cannot help returning on the same line, after whatever show of discussion and argument, because the line is already predetermined by the starting-point. The conclusion on the one side or the other is everywhere involved in the original terms of the question. "That which is born of the flesh is flesh; that which is born of the spirit is spirit." The Democritic philosopher, whether of the ancient or a modern school, is already a materialist--the Platonist already a Platonist--in the very language with which they respectively open their inquiries. All depends upon the presupposition as to what man is with which they set out.

The anthropological question, therefore, is really the primary question for all Philosophy, while the very possibility of a Theology hangs upon the answer given to it. If the answer be that of the modern scientific school, then the theological idea, or the idea of an extra-mundane sphere of which we can have any knowledge, disappears altogether. If nature round our life, and our processes of thought and action are all built up from without-the result, in their most subtle and lofty form, of material appliances-then anything beyond nature is imaginary. There is no room for the thought of God, or a sphere of divine action, or any element in us which derives meaning from this sphere. Theological dogmas vanish at a sweep, as a collection of mere shadows with which men have amused or tormented themselves. And this is clearly recognized by the modern scientific school, as an end at which they deliberately aim. Even earnest writers of this school have professed a wish that men would at length turn away from the contemplation of such shadows, and devote themselves to real work for the improvement of the world. What good might be done, they have virtually said, if only the intellectual enthusiasm and ability which are now wasted on theological questions were turned into the channel of scientific labour, and applied to the investigation of the realities of nature.[See [1]Appendix I.]

But the theological spirit is irrepressible. It rises from the very bosom of the school which disowns it, and takes new and strange shapes in its strange home. However man may prize science and its results, apparently he cannot live on them. There is that in him which demands something more. There are powers within him which remain restless and unsatisfied-conditions of morality and social order which seem unable to stay themselves save on eternal and divine laws.[1] The final answer to such questions as have again been raised respecting the very idea of religion must be sought in a renewed study of man's whole nature. What really is man in his complex activity? Can he be explained by reference to the mere laws of cosmical progress? Are the forces seen working endlessly in nature below him adequate to account for all his life? Or are there not forces in him unaccountable on this hypothesis, and which relate him to a higher sphere, just as really as his senses and other natural organs relate him to the lower sphere? Is he, in short, an animal, at the best, however noble an animal; and are Mr. Darwin and others in the true line of explaining not merely his physical but his emotional and moral activities by reference to the nascent germs of these in the lower animals? Does the idea of gradual development from below give the key not merely to a part but to the whole of his nature, although many links of the development are acknowledged to be still obscure? Or is there really a higher life in man-forces of morality, aspiration, and devotion which make him in creation a "singular effect"--the image of a reasonable Power higher than his own, who has made him, and to whom he is subject? Is mind, in short, prior to matter, and not its mere evolution? And is the higher life of man the expression of a Higher Mind that has endowed him with intelligence, morality, and capacity of worship?

John Tulloch, D.D.

It is impossible to get beyond this old antithesis lying at the foundation of all thought, and it is equally impossible to find a rational answer save in the study of man himself. If the naturalistic hypothesis can give an adequate account of man, then there is an end to the question. But not even the most extreme advocates of the hypothesis will venture to assert that they have approached the solution of man's mental, and still less of his moral, being along the line of lower life. Supposing that the fact of life were given them--and this in its very lowest forms they have failed to explain--they cannot confessedly find a passage from organic to conscious existence. The thread of evolution snaps asunder here. And even were they allowed to build on a basis of consciousness, they are powerless to erect thereon a moral structure. The moral life of humanity baffles all attempts to construct it merely from without. It is a kingdom within, unveiling itself from a higher source--as much a reality as the kingdom without, or the cosmos of natural law. Both, as Kant says, are equally true--"the starry heavens above and the moral law within;" [2] the former connecting itself with our external life, the latter revealing a faculty of life independent of animal, and even of all material existence. If there are times when we feel that the spiritual side of humanity has been somewhat exaggerated as an independent sphere, and an absolutism attributed to it which experience hardly warrants, there are other times when the whole strength of experience rises up against the most ingenious explanations of a psychological naturalism, and a sense of duty to a higher Power makes itself felt irresistibly. The heaven above is not more clear than the heaven of duty within. If we had to choose betwixt the two realities, the latter is the more intense and overpowering of the two.

But this may be admitted, and yet the Biblical idea be rejected. There are schools of thought in our time which emphasise the moral side of humanity, and yet reject the old religious background whence man as a moral intelligence was supposed to have come. They advocate strenuously a moral and even a religious nature in man, and go so far as to believe that human happiness can only be found in conformity to a religious ideal. But then they either deny the objectivity of this ideal altogether, or at least deny its old Biblical character as centring in a Divine Person, or an Intelligent and Holy Will ruling man and the world. Experience, it is allowed, gives the data of a higher life in man, just as surely as the data of a lower life. But then the higher life is either without any sphere beyond the visible and natural sphere which now encloses it, or the sphere which is above it and to which it answers is a mere dumb power or "stream of tendency," of which we can know nothing save that it is and that it acts. In this view morality is allowed, and religion is allowed and even warmly advocated. But neither the morality nor the religion are of the old Biblical type. They not only start with man, but they stay with man. The expression "God" may be used, but its meaning is entirely inverted. It no longer means a living Person outside of us,--an Intelligence to whom our intelligences can ascend and with whom they can communicate. It is merely an idealised abstraction of ourselves, or some impersonal Power and Law "not ourselves." In either case, and on every such hypothesis of making experience not merely the starting-point but the goal of religious thought, we can never pass into a higher or supernatural sphere of intelligence. To attempt this is to attempt Metaphysic; and all our modern schools of experience, whether they start from external nature and the generalisation of cosmical phenomena, or from man and the phenomena of moral conduct and aspiration, detest and disavow Metaphysic.

Nature and the facts of nature are tangible and powerful realities, say one class of our modern experience-philosophers--make what you can of them. If science and the laws which it unfolds are in themselves cold and uninspiring, clothe them with the ideas of sentiment and order. In other words, make them religion. It is contended by the special school of Positivists or the true Comtists that science must become religion, and it is their aim to preach as missionaries this new religion of scientific doctrine and scientific order. But to pass beyond the bounds of scientific generalisation is to pass into a region of nonsense. There is nothing, or at least nothing that we can ever know, beyond this region.

Others, again, virtually say, leave nature alone. It is the proper sphere of science, and a religion of science is hopeless. But look within, and there a new order of facts emerges as the true basis of religion. We know that to be good is better than to be bad; that righteousness is happiness: that in our life, in short, there is a moral order of whose existence we cannot doubt, any more than we can doubt of the existence of the outward cosmical order. Belief in the reality of this moral order is the essence of religion. The position seems Christian. It is put forth as the last or most modern expression of Christianity. [3] But it breaks down at the most vital point. For beyond the subjective sphere of moral experience it recognises nothing. To step beyond the moral order verifiable in our experience, to a Supernal order with a Supreme Intelligence at its head-this is no longer religion but theological Metaphysic, a mere region of chaos and wordy darkness in which we can verify nothing.

In neither of these cases is religion denied to man. On the contrary, the fullest concessions are made to it, and the line of experience is run out to its end, and possibly beyond its end. But in both alike all spiritual inference from the facts of experience is denied. Neither the cosmical order nor the moral order are held as witnessing to a Supreme Order, from which both come, and of which both are only the reflection. God (in the Biblical sense) is not only not the first word of these schools,--He is not their last. They not only do not take their authority from Him--they do not lead up to Him; He is not in all their thoughts. At the best and at the last there is only a glorified humanity, or "a power not ourselves making for righteousness." The measure of human experience is not only the measure of knowledge, but of being. Anthropology has not only taken precedence of Theology, but taken revenge upon it for its long neglect by extinguishing it. If a religion can be made out of man, and the facts that are verifiable in his experience,--good and well. But beyond the borders of this experience, to a single step of inference, or what they call inference, both the religions of science and of culture obstinately refuse to go.

But here again the question recurs, Do these anthropological religions (much as they repudiate Anthropomorphism, they are anthropological and nothing else) rightly interpret human nature, or give a true account of it? Is it possible, from a study of man himself, to rest satisfied either with a religion of cosmical law or of moral law? Are not those very facts of experience, of which so much is made, only intelligible in the light of a higher Supreme Law? Is all ethic not necessarily theologic, and do not the very ideas of right and wrong disappear apart from an Order which is not merely within man, but without him--a Supreme and Holy Will, from which all cosmical and moral activity alike flow, and to which they obediently return? Is not the moral life of humanity only conceivable as a reflected life, looking back towards this higher Source, and gathering all its true strength therefrom--a Source which has lifted it upwards through the ages, and drawn it always more near to its own Ideal? Is not humanity itself only intelligible as a created and not as a self-evolved personality; as a subject of education, and not of mere development; as the child of a Divine Father, and not the victim of a power not himself which punishes his unrighteousness? Is not the very conception of righteousness only reached by a moral sense or conscience in us, which, if it is allowed at all, witnesses to far more than a mere stream of tendency encompassing and controlling our lives?

In the course of these Lectures the views here indicated are everywhere implied. It was necessary, therefore, to make them so far clear at the outset. Our argument rests, and can only rest, both on a moral and a theistic basis. The question of sin is a question which has no existence save in the moral sphere. In the region of cosmical law it does not emerge at all. Whatever there may be of the appearance of evil within this sphere is either capable of explanation on an enlarged scientific view, or draws its character of mystery from the higher moral sphere which it touches. Apart from a moral law, enclosing all sentient life, and revealing itself as an intelligible and imperative guide in human life, there cannot even be the imagination of moral transgression. The most rudimentary conception of what is called sin vanishes. The fact of morality, therefore, and of a moral ideal, must be taken along with us from the outset.

But the fact of a metaphysical or theological sphere must no less be presumed. At the root, Metaphysic and Theology are one, and rest on the same basis; nay, Morality, in any true sense, appears to us to rest on no other basis. Otherwise it is only a generalisation of utilities without any permanent essence or unity. In man there is either a principle of life deeper than all nature (physis)--in other words, a metaphysical principle--or there is not. He is primarily either spiritual or material--a divinely-created soul, or a subtly-composed combination of mere physical elements, enclosing whatever variety of so-called spiritual experiences. There is no evading this final issue. The spiritual side of humanity, which in name is not denied by any school of thought with which it is necessary to argue, is either real in the old scholastic sense, or merely nominal--a growth from a divine root, transcending nature, and related to a Higher Spirit, which has implanted it; or it is a mere growth of nature, marvellously as it may have subtilised and purified the lower elements out of which it has grown. The latter alternative is that which is really assumed by all our modern schools, although less prominently by some than others. This is the meaning of their incessant assault and abuse of Metaphysic; of their equally incessant admiration and applause of experience. All the phases of mind and feeling, spiritual as well as sensible, are allowed for. These phases are facts to be woven into science and religion. But a metaphysical or spiritual ground in human nature an ens metaphysicum and soul--as a separate reality, with a separate and transcendent sphere of its own, is presumed to be mere superstition or delusion. The sphere of being is here and now--nowhere else. Soul is the finest experience ripened within this sphere; it is nothing else. But Metaphysic cannot be got rid of by mere assertion. The highest thought of every age has returned to a metaphysical basis, and found the only solution of its problems in the recognition of a sphere other than the present, and deeper than all phases of experience. Behind the phenomenal, in all its manifestations, it has found the noumenal--behind all the flow of experience, a unity of Divine Reason or Soul or Spirit in man, out of which alone have come the flower and fruit' of his higher life. It is of the essence of this higher life, not only that it is independent of matter, or springs from a source independent of matter, but that it is related to a world of spiritual or metaphysical reality--a supernatural order which everywhere touches it and conditions it. This supernatural order is no mere ideal rule or law--a projection of our higher imagination or an invasion of "something not ourselves," whence we cannot tell. It is a divine reality,--a Personal Reason and Will like our own, enlightening, educating, controlling us. Morality, in the true sense, is conformity to this divine reality; Philosophy, in the highest sense, is our theory of its mode of being; and Theology, our knowledge of its activities or manifestations. Alike they presuppose a transcendent or metaphysical basis. Let this basis be granted, all the rest follows. Let man himself be

John Tulloch, D.D.

Divine in his essential being, the theistic inference is a strict and legitimate one. Let this be denied, Theism disappears. The very idea of the Divine in the old, and, as we must hold, the only true sense, can never be reached.

Large, therefore, as may seem our assumptions to begin with, they all hang together. They come very much to the old Biblical truth that man is a created being, and not a mere result of natural development,--that he was made in the image of God, endowed with a reasonable will and conscience, and subject to the authority of the Divine Being who made him. The time was when it might have been a mere matter of course to start with such assumptions in treating any theological topic; but in the present atmosphere of opinion it is hardly possible to do this without at least indicating what we are doing, and, so to speak, clearing our path towards the special question which is to occupy us. It is only when we have planted ourselves on a spiritual or metaphysical basis, below all mere phases of experience, and brought ourselves face to face with Soul on the one hand and God on the other, subject and object alike transcending mere natural development, that our question comes into view at all. We cannot help, therefore, beginning on this basis, and implying it from the first. At the same time, we hope in the course of our exposition to do something to vindicate the soundness of such a basis. It will be found better than any other to harmonise with the results of our analysis of the profound enigma of sin. The enigma may remain insoluble; but if it be at all, it must cast some meaning on the true character of humanity. If man be a sinner, the fact of sin, however inscrutable it may remain in its own character, cannot fail to authenticate his spiritual origin and relationship, and thus throw back lines of proof in favour of the theistic conclusion with which we have started. This is not to reason in a circle, but only to bring back such truths as may be gathered in the recesses of our moral experience to light up the pathway along which we have travelled.

Having so far premised as to the character of the question before us in relation to modern schools of opinion, it still remains to consider as to our method of discussion. Sin being held to be a fact of human nature--an element of our moral consciousness--it might be thought best to begin with this consciousness, and to endeavour to fix the fact in the light of an internal analysis of its contents. If it be there, these contents must reveal it; and so we believe they do beyond doubt. Step by step the fact may be unfolded by an honest and searching scrutiny of the individual moral experience.

This is the method of analysis which is mainly followed by J. Müller in his great work on the Christian Doctrine of Sin, and it long appeared to us the true method of dealing with the subject,--first, to examine the individual consciousness in its inner witness to the fact--to draw out the features of this self-witness; and then to view the conclusions thus reached in the light of Scripture, especially of the significant statements on the subject in the apostolic writings. But this method no longer appears so satisfactory as it once did. It assumes too readily the fixity of the moral and religious consciousness in every individual. It makes this consciousness as it exists now, or in modern Christian nations, a standard of universal application. It assumes, moreover, that it is possible in some way to distinguish betwixt our natural and our inherited moral notions--our moral consciousness merely as human beings, and the same consciousness as informed and instructed by Divine Revelation. In the first instance, we are supposed to be dealing with the light of Nature, as if we were able to fix its elements apart by themselves, before we begin to contemplate them in the light of Scripture. But this is really an impossible task. The contents of Nature and Revelation cannot any longer be separated in this manner. The historic and the individual conscience are inextricably interwoven as cause and effect. We are all of us morally as well as intellectually what we are, not merely because of certain specific and typical endowments, but because of a long line of inherited experiences which have come to us from all past sources of culture, natural and revealed. We are born of Christian parents, and nursed from the first of Christian ideas, which have entered into the sources of our moral being, and given it both colour and substance. We cannot any longer discriminate in this being the specific from the general, the individual from the catholic compounds. What is ultimate in our higher thought can never be disentangled from our inheritance of belief and education. There is no doubt a certain morality and a certain religion in all men by nature. The history of ethics and the history of religion alike show this. If we go outside of Christianity, we still find man a creature of morality, or a subject of religion. This is enough to show that moral and religious instincts are a natural part of humanity. But, admitting this, it is no longer possible for those who have been educated within the long-descended line of Christian ideas, to determine clearly the elements either of a natural Ethic or a natural Religion as distinct from those ideas. They cleave to us too closely. Nay, they are so inwoven in the common fibre of our intellectual and spiritual life, that many of those who in our day assail Christianity with most intelligence and force, are found borrowing the very ideas with which they would supplant the Gospel from the atmosphere of morality which it has produced, and which without it would soon vanish. To this extent the modern idea of continuity must be admitted by all. The moral and religious life of humanity is a vast growth, which has taken up into its lifeblood all sources of past knowledge from Church and Scripture, as well as from Nature and Science. The light of so-called Nature and the light of Revelation have so mingled their rays in us, as to make up a blended experience which it is no longer possible to break up and refer to their respective sources.

The Christian Doctrine of Sin

It will be our aim, therefore, instead of beginning with the full idea of sin and appealing to Scripture everywhere for its proof, to review the idea in its gradual development. The idea is, according to our belief, a true one. It is verified by experience, recognised, described, and defined in Scripture. But, like all other ideas, it has grown from stage to stage in the human consciousness. It is not at first what it is afterwards--in its beginnings what it is in its full expression. It is now generally recognised that an idea is best understood and interpreted when thus unfolded along the whole line of its history--nay, that the best verification of the idea, or proof of its being true and not false, is just the manner in which it is seen from the beginning to cleave to the human mind and heart as a living possession.

Into this growth of religious ideas there enter all the factors which have been concerned in their production, expansion, or purification--not only the natural impulses of the human mind pushing onwards and realising more clearly its own powers, but also what is meant by Revelation, or the special introduction of new thoughts and impulses from a higher source. Without Revelation, religious ideas would never have been what they are. Hebrew and Christian monotheism, the great doctrines of the Trinity, the Incarnation, the Atonement, the doctrine of Sin in its full meaning, and Justification by grace, are all, according to Christian belief, the result of this higher communication. According to the same belief, they are true as thus communicated. But the higher source from which such ideas come does not destroy their capacity of growth. On the contrary, of all ideas the most living and fertile have been those of Revelation. They have been as a new power of life to the human consciousness, darkly growing up from the tangled weeds of its own superstitions to the clear light of God revealed in Christ. None of them were revealed in their fulness all at once. No doctrine has come forth in complete lineaments from the Divine mind. It has aggregated and acquired precision of outline from many influences working in the mind and heart of the Church in all ages. Theology exists for the purpose of analysing the aggregate, and elucidating and verifying the details of outline, and, in short, of presenting the doctrine in its full contents and meaning.

There is nothing novel in this view of Theology. I have not said there is. It has always been the business of Christian Theology to verify doctrine in the light of Scripture, and to trace how the various facts or texts of Scripture contribute to form the doctrine. But there is this difference betwixt the more recent and the older dogmatic method, that the modern theologian does not consider doctrines to be formed by a mere analysis and co-ordination of texts. They are not only logical deductions from Scriptural data; they are vital growths within the Christian consciousness. So the business of the theologian is not only to deduce conclusions from Scriptural premises, but to trace the vital links in the organism of Christian thought. He feels, moreover, the necessity of doing this in a true historic spirit; unfolding the doctrine from its first germ to its full outline; reading forward from the beginning, and not reading backward from the end, as has been so often done. This is what is meant by the historic method: not the discussion or estimate of past opinions, but the analysis from the first of a doctrine in its vital growth in the human consciousness. The modern theologian desires to look at the genesis of Christian ideas' as far as possible in their own light; to see them as they grow, and not merely to handle them as past logical forms. He may fail in this. Misconceptions will cling to him in spite of himself; and he will look at the past in the light of the present, and judge it thereby. But at any rate he has breathed the new historic atmosphere which surrounds the modern intelligence, and he feels that the end is not as the beginning in doctrine any more than in anything else; that there is a continuous movement all along the line of its development; and that his proper business is not to carry back the fullness of the result to measure the first springs of the movement, but to study these springs as they rise in their first freshness, and to trace, with unforced and discriminating intelligence, their gradual advance till they swell into the full dogmatic utterance of the Church.

A confusion of the spheres of what have hitherto been called Nature and Revelation [See [2]Appendix IV.] may seem to follow from this view. We have already spoken of the difficulty of discriminating these spheres in our own experience; and the extreme schools of religious opinion, both in this country and in Holland and Germany, willingly confuse them, and recognise nothing essentially distinctive in what we call Revelation. Yet there is nothing in the conception itself, or the method which has grown out of it, that necessitates this confusion. Both factors--the natural and supernatural, the human and the divine--are alike present in the formation of all religious thought. It may be impossible always to distinguish them; it is to us certainly impossible, at this stage of religious progress, to discriminate the elements either of a natural Ethic or a natural Religion separable from the course of Christian ideas, and self-authenticating on a basis of its own. The historic method has destroyed these presumptions of a former Deism, which tried vainly to stand aloof from the course of Christian intelligence. But, in doing so, it is so far from having destroyed the claims of Nature on the one hand, or Revelation on the other, that it has carried them up into a living unity of Christian Reason, or of Reason informed and enlightened by all the influences, higher and lower, divine and natural, which have nurtured and fashioned it from the beginning.

I shall endeavour, therefore, in these Lectures, to treat first the growth of the idea of evil, in its most general aspect, as it meets us in those forms of religious culture which preceded or were entirely outside of that divine education of the Hebrew race under which the special consciousness of sin was developed. This will bring before us the only purely "natural" notions on the subject-the workings of the human mind and feeling regarding it, untouched by any special revelation.

I shall then pass to consider the idea of evil as apprehended by the Hebrew mind, or the rise and progress in that mind of the idea of sin, under the special divine training to which it was subjected. I shall treat, in other words, of the Old Testament doctrine of sin, which is absolutely necessary to the understanding of the developed doctrine in the New Testament.

This fully developed doctrine will next engage us under the several significant aspects in which it took hold of the primitive Christian consciousness as represented in the New Testament Scriptures, especially as depicted in the Gospels and the Epistles of St. Paul. The doctrine of original sin, as the final expression of the Christian consciousness in the apostolic or first Christian age, will finally occupy us and close our present exposition.

There are endless collateral controversies as to moral freedom, the nature and extent of the moral law, the relation of sin in its origin to the human and divine will, set forth in various theories. But I shall endeavour to keep as close to the subject as I can. There is little good in following the inquiry into regions which transcend all experience and all means of reaching a verifiable conclusion, or in beating out the straw of old controversies which have lost all or most of their meaning. It is unnecessary to entangle ourselves with the thoughts of others, save where they bear directly upon our line of exposition. The subject, as thus sketched, is ample and interesting enough in itself to occupy our whole space.

Footnotes:

1. Megas en toutois theos oude geraskei.--Soph., O. T., 871.

2. Kritik der praktischen Vernunft, quoted by Sir W. Hamilton in his Lectures on Metaphysics, p. 39, 40. See passage in [3]Appendix II.

3. Dr. Matthew Arnold's position is so well known by his recent works that it is unnecessary to do more than refer to it. But the same position is virtually held by the influential school of divines, known as the "modern school," in Holland. See in [4]Appendix III. an interesting statement of their position.

II – IDEA OF EVIL OUTSIDE OF REVELATION

THE question of evil is as old as humanity itself. It enters into all forms of religion. It is the background of mystery in all human life; and its shadow falls over that outward world of cosmical law which seems most removed from it.

Amidst the pervading harmonies of creation there are forces ready to break forth with destructive activity, and to spread around ruin and disaster. Nature is powerful for harm as well as for help, a storehouse of death as well as of life. [See [5]Appendix V.] Darkness and storm alternate with light and serenity; the peaceful courses of the seasons are interrupted by the incalculable fury of the tempest; and even the security of the abiding earth and heavens seems invaded by the explosions of the earthquake and the ominous gloom of the eclipse. These phenomena may be all equally ordered, but they powerfully excite the suggestion of evil in the human imagination. In primitive times they touch it with a peculiarly vivid force of apprehension and dread; and even after the light of science has searched the secrecies of Nature, and laid bare its wondrous order everywhere, there lingers in the popular mind a deep distrust of all unwonted phenomena.

In the region of sensitive life the idea of evil presents itself directly. Here it is that Nature is "red in tooth and claw," [4] and its very arrangements seem designed not merely to produce good, but to inflict evil. The whole range of animal existence presents a mingled scene of enjoyment and suffering--a scene bright with the activities of life, and health, and triumph, but also dark with the endurance of weakness, terror, and violence, the latter apparently entering into the constitution of the animal world as immediately as the other.

And when we turn to the highest form of life in man himself, the presence of evil haunts it everywhere in endless forms of general and individual experience in all relations of human society, all functions of human industry, and in the noblest energies of human progress. We cannot conceal its working when we look within our own hearts. Nay, here more than anywhere it shows its deepest power, and touches human experience with acutest misery. Different natures will apprehend differently the depth and power of evil in human life; but there are none, not even the most sentimental enthusiasts, call dispute its existence; and it requires only a slight degree of moral earnestness to be solemnly arrested by it. The highest natures have been most moved by its mystery; and those who have most realised the greatness of man, and done most for his good, have at the same time felt most pathetically the shadows of evil that rest upon his lot.

So far there can hardly be any difference of opinion as to the fact which we call evil. Whatever men may make of the fact, its presence around them, and in their own life, admits of no denial.

A fact so universal and so painful, touching human life at all points with such a sore pressure, has been necessarily a subject of much inquiry and reflection. Men have never ceased interrogating the mystery which lies around them and within them. The history of religion is in great part a history of the explanations which men have tried to give of it. It is the business of these Lectures to deal with one of these explanations. The Christian answer to the question of evil, apart from all considerations of its essential importance, is one which can never cease to interest all thoughtful minds. It is at least one of the most intelligible and consistent that has been given. But, before entering upon our special task, it will be well to bring under brief review such answers as have occurred to the human mind in its successive stages of religious progress. The course of religious thought outside the Jewish and the Christian Revelation may, or may not, be the product of purely natural reflection. Elements of primeval tradition may mingle in it; but, at least, it is the only source whence we can gather the contents of Natural Religion in any intelligible sense of these words.

It is needless to say that we make no attempt to handle this part of our task with historical completeness. Any such attempt would lead us far into the wide field of comparative Theology. [See [6]Appendix VI.] No field of inquiry can be more interesting; but it is beyond our present scope, as it is beyond our knowledge. All that we propose to do is to trace rapidly the chief ideas of evil that meet us in the great world of religious thought--unrepresented by the Jewish or Christian Scriptures. Such a sketch, however rapid, if at all intelligent, can hardly fail to throw a reflected light on the Christian doctrine, and to bring into bolder and more precise relief its distinguishing features. In point of fact it will be found that the answers which have been given to the problems of evil outside of revelation run in a few main lines, which continually repeat themselves, and which seem to exhaust all the efforts of human speculation on the subject.

Glancing, then, at the world of religious thought outside of Christianity and its anticipatory revelation, we may be said to meet with the following successive developments of the idea of evil-some of them of the nature of reasoned or speculative solutions, others in the main unconscious generalisations which have dominated human intelligence, without professing to unravel the mystery which it faces.

1. The rudest conception of evil is that which meets us in prehistoric and savage religions. [See [7]Appendix VII.] It is the instinct of the savage to conceive of the external world as upon the whole evil rather than good. No intelligence can be said to mingle with this instinct or to guide it. It is only a crude confused sense in the mind of the savage of the pressure of natural forces upon his security, comfort, or possessions. What is evil, and still less what is good, in any deeper sense, he never asks himself. He is incapable of even forming coherent imaginations of the one or the other; but instinctively he trembles before a Power or Powers which can hurt him, blight the fruits of his labour or destroy his cattle, deny his success in the chase and triumph in war; and he offers rites or uses spells or incantations to drive away these Powers, or draw them to his side. The evil is therefore truly far more of a god to him than the good, and devil-worship, however revolting and unintelligible to a later reflectiveness, is only a natural inference of the savage view of life and of Nature. So radical is the hold which evil in some form or another has over the human heart and imagination.

2. As we pass to the earliest forms of historical religion, a higher and better view of Nature meets us. It is still full of evil, but it is also full of good. Its great contrasts of light and shade, of beauty and terror, are reproduced and personified. The external world continues to dominate the religious imagination; but this world is no longer a mere repertory of evil powers ready to crush man or destroy the fruits of his labour. It is a scene of incessant activity, productiveness, and life. The clear sky above, the radiant sunlight, the sweet wind no less than the destructive blast, fire, water, earth, all that is joyful as well as all that is gloomy in the great picture of the outward world, are idealised and clothed in imaginary forms. There may be no depth of intelligence, no clear lines drawn even betwixt natural qualities; yet the one side of the picture is given as well as the other. The brighter side is often given as the more prominent of the two.

There is great variety in the forms of religion which occupy this stage of development. The wide group of polytheistic faiths which meets us in the earliest centres of civilisation of which we have any record may be said to belong to it. Some of them are greatly more advanced than others, and rise at points into a region of pure moral conception; but in their origin all may be said to rest on a dual imagination of nature, and none of them quite outreach the conditions of their origin.

The religion of ancient Egypt, supposed by some to represent a more primitive stratum of religious idea than any Aryan or Semitic faith, is a conspicuous example of the rudest form of this embodiment of Nature-force in contrasted types of good and evil. In this as in all Nature-religions, the sun under various names is the great type of the Good--the symbol of joyous activity and beneficence. Evil, again, is pictured in the darkness of night, the cold of winter, or the devastating heat of summer. Osiris seems to gather to himself in the later Egyptian mythology all the higher qualities of active goodness, while Isis is the correspondent passive or receptive principle. Beside these stands Typhon the evil principle, conspicuous as powerful, able to slay Osiris and banish him to the region of the dead, but not able to detain him there. Sought after by Isis, he is found and brought back to life again, as the sun rises again after the darkness of the night. The Evil stands beside the Good, and enters into conflict with it, but it no longer fills the imagination.

The religions of Phoenicia and of the older civilisations which spread around the valley of the Euphrates present a similarly rude deification of Nature-force. The Baal of Phoenicia is now good and now evil--now Baal-Adonis and now Baal-Moloch. Ashera, or Astarte, the female divinity, is also partly good and partly evil; now the symbol of joy and grace and beauty, in which aspect she seems to be cognate with the Hellenic Aphrodite and the Ephesian Diana, and now the symbol of terror and grossness. Adonis, torn by a bloody boar, and again reappearing to the light, is the same myth as Osiris killed by Typhon--the Good overcome by the Evil, but not conquered by it. The higher principle regains its ascendancy, and takes its position in front of the other.

In all these conceptions, obviously the Good and Evil are alike drawn from Nature; but there is some movement of thought if not of moral interest. The human intellect has grown, if not to understand Nature, yet not merely to be afraid of it. Everywhere it sees two sides,--light as well as shade-- brilliancy, life, and abundance, as well as negation, sterility, and darkness. Nature is no longer formless or merely evil; there is a rude, if incoherent, attempt at classification. Mere blind wonder and fear have ceased, and the mind recognises and symbolises the Good no less than the Evil. The conceptions are cloudy and interchangeable, but they are there. The first step in the great movement of religious thought has begun.

The Vedic and Hellenic mythologies mark the greatest advance in this stage of religious thought; and in the latter particularly, the stage outruns itself into the moral sphere. Primarily, however, both mythologies start with Nature. The gods of India and of Greece, no less than of Egypt, are impersonations of natural force. Indra is the symbol of the Sun--of the serene sky--"who makes the lightning to spring forth and launches the light." The clouds that darken the sky represent the powers of evil that fight against Indra. They march under the guidance of Vritra, or "that which obscures." Again, the swift winds which chase the clouds are the auxiliaries of Indra, and the two first rays of the morning are twin divinities, traversing the heaven in a rapid car, and scattering in their passage fecundity and life. Varuna (Heaven), Indra (Light), Agni (Fire), are all in turn represented as the great Nature-force and supreme Power. The hymns celebrate them simultaneously; and each, without relation to the other, seems to occupy the chief place. "The whole mythology," as Max Müller says, "is fluent." The powers of Nature stand alongside of one another rather than in subordination to one another. They are idealisations of natural force, and yet they take to themselves moral attributes, and clothe themselves at times with a gracious and divine personality. It is hardly possible to excel the moral spirit of some of the Vedic hymns, as, for example, the following: "Let me not yet, O Varuna, enter into the house of clay. Have mercy, Almighty; have mercy. Through want of strength, thou strong and bright God, have I gone to the wrong shore. Have mercy, Almighty; have mercy. Whenever we seem, O Varuna, to commit an offence--whenever we break thy law through thoughtlessness--have mercy, Almighty; have mercy." [5]

This moral growth is still more conspicuous in the Homeric mythology. The Zeus of Homer is not merely the Vedic Indra--the sun vanquishing darkness; but he is a father and king--the source of moral order, the judge of domestic right. Pallas is not merely the brightness of the serene sky, but the reflection of thought--the source of prudence, eloquence, art, and wit. Apollo is the symbol at once of light and of purity--the Hellenic messenger or Messiah mediating betwixt heaven and earth; [See [8]Appendix VIII.] and even Aphrodite, one of the least moral of the Hellenic divinities, is not merely the impersonation of voluptuous beauty, but of all bewitching softness and poetic grace, as she rises from the foam of the Cytherean wave.

But admitting all this, it is none the less true that the most perfect of these conceptions have not only their origin in Nature, but that they never completely rise above it; the vesture of their birth everywhere clings to them. The moral conception is never clearly marked off from the unmoral or even the immoral; the one passes into the other. Even the personal conception sinks back into Nature and loses itself ever and again in the vast and dim realm of the cosmos. Human reflectiveness has greatly advanced, and stands face to face with Nature, no longer in mere dread, nor yet in a mere twofold vision of darkness and light. The darkness, indeed, has almost vanished from the scene. The Evil has lost its power by losing its grossness; it lies hidden away behind the bright creation of that wonderful Olympus. But it is only hidden away. There was such a sunlight in the early Greek imagination that it suffused all the activities of Nature and of life by its glow; but the gloomy shadows lay in wait behind even the glowing Epos. Olympus itself rested on a dark realm of night and chaos, and the gloom of Hades haunted the hero amidst all his cheerful toils and perils. Nowhere, certainly, in all human history, does the conception of evil play a less powerful part than in the early Greek religion, yet even here it is not banished. It is the formless background out of which rises alike the cosmos of natural beauty and the glory of the heroic life. Moral qualities mingle in the latter and touch it with a splendour more than that of earth, but Nature imprisons and limits both the Good and the Evil. Far as in special traits they may rise above it, they still return to the soil which nurtured them, and which conditions their highest aspirations.

3. It is in a different quarter to which we must look for the first definite growth of a moral conception of evil, or of such a marked separation betwixt the Good and Evil as to place them in direct antagonism. Early in the unknown history of the Aryan tribes, but subsequent to their final dispersion eastwards and westwards, there seems to have occurred, in the primitive home of the race, something of the nature of a religious revolution. The symbolism of Nature, with its tendency to assume a polytheistic shape, and to obscure moral distinctions, must have become unsatisfactory, and led to a strong reaction in some higher mind or minds who had power to turn the popular religious thought in a new and more spiritual direction. The old antagonisms of light and darkness, of sunshine and storm, became transformed, as Bunsen says, [6] into antagonisms of good and evil--of Powers exerting a beneficent or corrupting influence on the mind. The old Aryan nomenclature underwent a singular change. The terms remained, but received a reversed significance. The appellation of the good powers was applied to the powers of evil. Dævas, for example--cognate with Deva and Dyaus, the name of God, the supreme type of light or the serene sky, the Heaven-Father--came to denote the spirits of evil, or the genii of darkness who fight under the Prince of Darkness.

The author of this remarkable revolution in Aryan thought is generally known as Zoroaster, or Zarathustra, as the name is more correctly written. But beyond the fact of such a name, and the religion connected with it, nothing can be said to be distinctly ascertained. All attempt to construct Persian any more than Egyptian chronology and history seems hopeless. The era of Zarathustra, according to different writers, varies from about 600 B.C. to 1000 B.C., or even a much earlier date. Most scholars entitled to express an opinion on the subject believe that he cannot be placed later than the second-mentioned of these dates. But not only is the date of Zarathustra uncertain, doubts have even been cast upon his personality. It has been suggested that the name may stand, not for an individual, but for a school of early Aryan prophets, who initiated the great change of religious thought which has descended to us under the title of Zoroastrianism.

The uncertainty which hangs around the origin of the system cannot be said to attach to the system itself. It is a distinctly-conceived dualism, in which the physical contrasts presented by pre-existing religions have become almost entirely merged in moral antagonism. Man is represented as surrounded by good and evil spirits, ranged under respective leaders--Ormuzd or Ahura-Mazda, the Holy-minded, and Ahriman or Anra-Mainyus, the Evil-minded. These spiritual powers wage with each other an incessant war, and man has to make his choice betwixt them. He cannot serve two masters. He must choose the one and reject the other. The Good Power is represented as the Creator. "I worship and adore," says Zarathustra, "the Creator of all things, Ahura-Mazda, active Creator, . . . Lord of the worlds--Lord of good things, . . . the first fashioner--who made the pure creation." [7] And yet Evil is supposed to be also an independent power from the beginning--having a coequal existence with the Good. "In the beginning there was," says the prophet, "a pair of twins--two spirits, each having his own distinct essence. These, the Good and the Evil, rule over us in thought, word, and deed." [8] And. the difficulty of the choice betwixt good and evil rests just in this, that the one holds man as really, and, so to speak, as rightfully, as the other.

It is unnecessary to dwell upon the marked development of thought which this system exhibits. Good and Evil are so far plainly transferred from the region of Nature to the region of Spirit. The evil is not that which merely hurts, or weakens, or destroys man. It is not merely the gloom of night or the fury of the desolating storm, as in Vedism; or the pale dread of an unknown future, as in Hellenism. Good and Evil are nowhere seen interchanging, or lying in indiscriminate confusion alongside one another. But Evil is from the first a spiritual power behind nature, and operating primarily upon the mind and heart. It is twin with the Good; and through the necessary encounter of the two all things are brought about--the world of life is formed. But, twin in being and in the genesis of the world, they are wholly opposed in character. Veracity, purity, righteousness, are the attributes of the one; lies, uncleanness, and destructiveness are the qualities of the other. In short, the sphere of Nature, which we have seen to bound even the loftiest conceptions of the Homeric pantheon, is almost entirely left behind in this remarkable system. We have passed from the outward to the inward--from the cosmical, not merely to the personal, but to the ethical.

Yet when we look more closely, there are traces here also of the aboriginal soil out of which all Nature-religions have grown. Good is not wholly spiritual, or Evil either. A dead body is as polluted as a lie; and a fine field of wheat is as pleasing in the sight of Ahura-Mazda as a purified conscience. It is obvious, further, how the very conception of Evil as twin with Good, and equally independent with it, serves so far to destroy its moral character. That which is an inherent and necessary power in the creation of the world cannot be an essential contradiction of its highest law. Rather it must enter into all created things as their true complement and condition. There are passages from the Zend-Avesta which seem to rise above this necessary dualism or essential twofoldness of evil as well as good in the composition of the world. Bunsen and others have at least drawn a higher meaning from these passages. But there can be little doubt that Persian religious thought never surmounted the fundamental dualism on which it is based, and which has been so prominently identified with it. Some of the nobler Gâthâs, or hymns of the Persian scriptures, may speak of the world as divine, or of the Good Spirit ruling us all; but in others the Evil Spirit claims to rank alongside of the Good. And it was the fate of Zoroastrianism to plant the dualistic conception so deep in the human consciousness, that it is seen constantly reappearing in the subsequent history of religious thought, and even within the sphere of Christianity itself.

Nothing, indeed, is more remarkable than the vitality of this conception. It is the definite basis, if not of all Gnostic thought, of those special forms of it which were allied to Orientalism, and which are sometimes spoken of as branches of the Syrian in contrast to the Alexandrian Gnosis. The question of evil, of its origin and its relation to the Supreme Being, was the great question of Gnosticism; and the solution which it gave of the question from one point of view was plainly borrowed from Zoroastrianism. It imagined the Demiourgos, or creator of the natural world, to be an actively malignant or evil being at war with the Supreme--an Ahriman in conflict with the absolute Source of life and goodness. There was this difference--a difference so far in favour of the original system--that in all the phases of Gnosticism the higher Divine Principle is conceived as infinitely apart from the work of creation, abiding in an exclusive supremacy. It is the Evil that is creative or demiurgic, and not the Good. The two are not coactive, but the Evil is, so to speak, the only activity invading the passive sphere or abyss of Being. A latent Pantheism, in short, lurks in all Gnostic thought, of which there is no trace in primitive Zoroastrianism. Yet the dualistic stands in front of the pantheistic conception, and probably gave to the various forms of the Syrian Gnosis its popular hold upon many minds in the first Christian ages.

The Christian Doctrine of Sin

In the third century Dualism took fresh life and burst forth with new momentum under the name of Manichæism. This system especially emphasised the power of Evil as a distinct and coeternal principle in antagonism with the Good. [9] It acquired a rapid ascendancy, and exercised more influence than any preceding systems of the same character. In the fourth and fifth centuries it paraded itself as almost a rival of Christianity. Augustine was for a time its disciple, and speaks of its great teacher, Faustus, with all his superficiality and lack of precise thought, as a man of eloquence and influence. But even this great outburst of dualistic speculation by no means exhausted its vitality. It sprang up again suddenly in the East in the twelfth century, founding a new sect under the name of Paulicians, who seem somehow to have identified their characteristic principles with the teaching of St. Paul. Gibbon has given, in the fifty-fourth chapter of this great history, an animated description of this sect, and of the rapidity with which it spread, notwithstanding violent persecution, through Bulgaria and the borders of the Greek empire into Italy, Germany, and France. "It was discovered," he says, "that many thousand Catholics of rank and of either sex had embraced the Manichæan heresy" [10] (under this new name). The heresy spread, especially in the south of France; and there, amongst other uncatholic opinions, filled up the measure of heterodoxy and contempt for sacred forms which called forth and consecrated the horrors of the Albigensian war. It can hardly be said that even in modern times this old conception has lost its power, when we find one great philosopher writing of another--Mr. J. S. Mill of his father--"that he found it impossible to believe that a world so full of evil was the work of an author combining infinite power with perfect goodness and righteousness;" but that he by no means discredited in the same degree "the Sabæan and Manichæan theory of a Good and an Evil Principle struggling against each other for the government of the universe." [11]

4. The conception of evil was destined to undergo still further modifications outside the sphere of Judaism and Christianity. The original worship of the Aryan race, which under the influence of a noble inspiration passed into the ethical ardour of Zoroastrianism, became transformed on another side, first into the sacerdotal pantheism of Brahmanism, and then into the philosophy of Buddha, which has received various interpretations, but which, in all its interpretations, more or less implies the same conception of evil. It is no part of our work to trace these developments of religious thought flowing from the same fountain-head, partly revolutionary and partly reactionary in their relation to one another. All that it concerns us to note is, that the idea of evil, which is very prominent in both, is quite different from that clearly-defined personality which meets us in the Zoroastrian or Irano-Persian system of which we have been speaking. There the world of created life--man and all things--share in the Evil which, no less than the Good, has been concerned in their production. But while sharing in evil as an essential element of his being, man is at the same time invited to active struggle with it. He has the choice of the Good or the Evil, and all his higher activities are evoked to overcome the one and embrace the other. The Kingdom of Darkness holds him within its sphere, and the Prince of Darkness rules him by right, so to speak, of joint property; yet there appears to be a sphere within the conditions of his present life where the evil may be vanquished. The pious heart is promised the inheritance of the earth.[12] The struggle here, therefore, is not hopeless, and human life may be glorified in deliverance from evil. But when we turn to Brahmanism, we find that evil is no longer merely present in life--no longer merely claims a joint share in it--but has, in fact, become its characteristic condition. Existence itself, or at least conscious existence, has become the Evil. It is no longer a fight against an evil power; it is itself evil. To have passed from the infinite to the finite--from unconsciousness to consciousness--to have been born into this world of change at all, is evil. There is, accordingly, not merely evil in the world, concerned in its production, holding its own in its government, but the world is evil itself, and the mere fact of life is a fall from true Being and Good.

This may seem a strange outcome of the lively Nature-worship of the Aryan tribes, as depicted in the hymns of the Rig-Veda. But it seems to have been a natural consequence of the changes which passed upon the race as they went eastward, settling in the valley of the Ganges, and exchanging their nomadic and warlike character for a pacific and settled social state. Surrounded by luxuriant and gigantic forms of nature, and under a comparatively unchanging sky, they seem to have lost their natural activity both of life and imagination. Their bards, as Bunsen says, "gradually became a guild which shaped itself into a priestly caste." [13] Their versatile and joyous symbolism of Nature degenerated into a sacerdotal system, in which Indra and his cognate divinities passed out of notice, and Brahma took their place. Apparently at first a mere abstract name for the contemplation of what was "sacred" or "holy," this word came to denote (in a neuter form [14]) the Divine, the Eternal--in opposition to the temporal, the phenomenal--and also (in a masculine form) the God of the Brahmans, or the chief God of the later Hindu mythology. The idea of Brahma, however, even as a distinct object of worship, remained very impersonal, and never acquired any hold of the popular mind. He is nowhere so much a personality as a Universal Soul or Spirit of the world, of which all finite things are the manifestation. "The Universe is Brahma, it proceeds from Brahma, [15] and is finally again absorbed by Brahma." Brahma is Being, pure Being; all else is his word or image. But in so far as Being has passed into Form, and the Eternal clothed itself with the temporal, and the Infinite become the finite, evil has arisen. To be out of Brahma in any sense is so far evil. "The cycle of the universe is an error;"[16] Brahma is the only reality. "Thou, I, the universe must pass away;"[17] Brahma alone abides, "without dimension, quality, character, or duality."[18] "A wise man must annihilate all objects of sense in his mind, and contemplate continually only the one Mind which is like pure space."[19]

It is unnecessary to dwell upon the vast change which has passed upon Aryan thought in the elaboration of such a system as this, and how entirely it transfers us to a new point of view regarding evil. In one sense it might seem an advanced point of view. It is the result of a more distinct effort of thought--a more meditative philosophy. The Dualism of the Zoroastrian is a more spontaneous suggestion than the Pantheism of the Brahman--an older and so to speak a rougher and more popular type of thought. But the Brahmanical conception of evil, later as it is in its development and more profound in mystery, is really not an advance upon the Zoroastrian conception; rather it is a degeneracy. The moral import which we were able to trace everywhere in the one has quite gone out of the other. There can be no genuine moral sphere in an existence which is evil by the mere fact that it is at all; whose very creaturely beginning is a fall from the Divine, and whose only salvation is a return to it, not by any moral effort or renovation, but by re-absorption. This--the only Good--stood at an infinite distance from the creature, whose destiny it was to pass from one form of life to another, conditioned by the preceding. The doctrine of Metempsychosis crowned the Brahmanic system, and contributed to render it one of the most mournful and oppressive of all religions. Life was not only evil in its present consciousness, but there opened before it a series of changes all more or less evil, from which there was no escape but by losing all individuality, and perishing in the abyss of pure Being.

So far, Buddhism was a reaction against all this oppressive sense of misery in life. It taught, in opposition to the apparently endless law of transmigration, and the sacerdotalism which made capital out of this law, that happiness was to be found in a life of conscious virtue, and that religion was not a system of rites and ceremonies, but a true order of reverence, and charity, and self-denial. "To conquer one's self is a greater victory than to gain a battle." "He who for only one moment contemplates himself in utter repose"--"who cherishes reverence for the virtuous"--this one act of devotion is better than a hundred years' sacrifices. "To refrain at all times from angry words, and never to do another injury; to observe temperance; to live in profoundest meditation,--lo! this is enjoined in the Buddhas.'[20] Sayings such as these, which are to be found without number in the Buddhist scriptures, are sufficient to prove the high moral tone of Buddhism, and the extent to which it formed a reformation of the Brahmanical system, which, like the Pharisaism of the Gospels, had become intolerable to many pious hearts. But, not to speak of deeper defects, Buddhism, with all its strenuous culture of moral life, never rose above the degrading conception of existence as a whole presented in the older faith. It preached the divinity of virtue, the negation of desire, the beauty of repose. It tried to clear a space within the present life for the exercise of reverence, and purity, and charity, and honorable obedience. "He who cherishes reverence in his heart, and ever honours his superiors, to him shall be ever added these four gifts--long life, beauty, joy, power."[21] But withal, it left life as a natural fact under the curse of evil. Of the four sublime verities, the first is that "existence is suffering,"--and the second, that the cause of the suffering is desire or sensation. There is a sense, indeed, in which these Buddhistic aphorisms might bear a Christian meaning. There might seem little to choose betwixt the well-known language of Job and the words of the Buddha proverb, "Man's birth is full of trouble, and full of toil is his life also;"[22] and "He that loseth his life shall find it,"--"Whoso loveth father and mother better than me," might seem to find their echo in the divine honour attributed in another proverb to him "who, loose from all human ties, has risen to the divine communion."[23] But the spiritual standpoint is vitally different in the two cases. The life of sense, the life of affection, even the life of thought on its active, speculative, or scientific side, is all more or less evil from the Buddhistic point of view. Perfection--Nirvâna--however we may specially interpret the word, is only to be attained by self-contemplation, and in the end by ecstacy. Good, in short, only arises in so far as life in all its actualities is left behind. "The greatest happiness, is not to be born; the next greatest is for those who have been born to die soon." Even according to Bunsen, who has found a higher divine meaning in Buddhism than many others, this was its final dogma. The curse of evil clung to all sense of individual being. Bliss was only reached by annihilating all the conditions of relative existence, and plunging into Nirvâna--the Void--or, so far as can be understood, into Annihilation.[24]

If the Dualism of the Irano-Persian faith perpetuated itself in certain forms of Gnosticism, the conception of evil as material existence was no less persistent in the speculation of succeeding ages. It may be questioned whether Brahmanism or Buddhism exerted any direct influence upon Alexandrian philosophy, or the successive forms of what is known as Neo-Platonism. But there can be no doubt that it was the same thought which repeated itself in those speculations. Evil was identified with finite being, or matter per se. Existence of itself simply was conceived of as a descent from the Divine. The idea of emanation, which underlay both the great oriental systems, was no less characteristic of the Alexandrian Gnosis in all its branches. The Infinite or pure Being was the only reality--all else was but as the shadow or manifestation of the Primal Source; and in the progress of descent from this source, evil emerged so soon as the fontal stream of spiritual life touched matter. Every successive evolution of the divine element grew feebler till it ended in opposition to the Divine. Matter and its adjuncts--sensation, desire, bodily affections of whatever kind--were all more or less at variance with the Divine, and therefore to be resisted as evil. It is needless to point out how pervading this thought has been, not only in Gnosticism and various forms of medieval mysticism, but throughout the whole history of monasticism, and even many practices of ordinary Christian devotion. It has been the latent spring of Christian asceticism in all its branches. Evil in such cases may not have been exclusively traced to matter, but it has been more or less associated with it; and the way to be good has been supposed to lie through self-mortification and the triumph of the spirit over the desires of the body. The Buddhist doctrine of the annihilation of self, extravagant as it may appear when stated in its nakedness, has a deep root in human nature; and the thought of evil only passing away when all self-feeling has been lost in the Divine, reappears in almost every phase of exalted religious feeling. It may receive a purely spiritual interpretation; but it is also apt to pass into externality, and to confound wrong with certain aspects of the natural life. The activities of natural healthfulness, the joys of sense, the joys even of the domestic hearth--whatever intensifies the mundane aspects of existence--come to be regarded with suspicion as partaking more or less of the lower or material sphere of being. All connected with this sphere is more or less of the nature of evil. The Good is only reached in the negation of nature, and in a supposed spiritual elevation of feeling which leaves far behind all mere joys of earth. And so it often happens that a mysticism which claims in its very loftiness to be peculiarly Christian, falls back by its excess into the Buddhistic or Gnostic Error of considering matter and its adjuncts as the source of evil. Manifold as are the forms of error, its range of development lies along two or three main lines; and these lines are seen constantly repeating themselves, sometimes in the most unexpected quarters.

5. We have spoken of the idea of Evil in the early Hellenic religion as. lying alongside the Good in unconscious simplicity. Zeus is the father of gods and men, and yet the faithless husband. The free-hearted Achilles hates concealment. Ulysses is commended for his clever powers of deceit. The moral idea has not worked itself clear from the vague indiscriminate aspects of nature or of life in which "all things come alike to all: there is one event to the righteous, and to the wicked; to the good, and to the clean, and to the unclean." [25] But Hellenic thought, it is necessary to remember, is a great history of itself. It passes through many stages; and in the course of its development the idea of evil becomes greatly deepened, and the conception of a Nemesis or moral order rises within it, if not so purely, yet almost as conspicuously and majestically as in the Hebrew Prophets. The chief sphere of this development is the Greek Tragedy. Behind all the activities of life, and all the play of dramatic passion which compose this Tragedy, there is a stern background of Righteousness which will by no means clear the guilty. A shadowy terror overhangs all wrongdoing, and a curse which cannot be turned away pursues the offenders. This moral background is the great inspiring ideal of the Greek drama, and lends to it its chief grandeur and power. The ideal, in its mere force of awe and majesty, may be said to rival that of Hebrew thought; but in other and essentially moral respects it falls below it. The sphere of moral freedom is recognised but dimly; the distinction betwixt voluntary and involuntary evil comes forth but darkly and hesitatingly. Nemesis is just, but with a justice that spares not; and the darkness of a sublime despair settles on the awful scenes of human crime and misery. The moral elevation of Greek Tragedy, and the contrasts of right and wrong which it sets forth, are the highest and gravest efforts of Gentile thought in a religious direction. They bring us to the very verge of Revelation, but they do not pass within it. And deep and sad, tender and pathetic, as are its pictures of human life and heroic duty, the idea of evil which enters into it so largely is yet far short of the idea of sin which emerges on the very threshold of the Hebrew Scriptures.

Footnotes:

    4. In Memoriam, LVI.

    5. Hymn to Varuna (Rig. vii. 89), translated by Max Müller, Chips from a German Workshop,' i. 39.

    6. God in History, i. 273.

    7. Substance of hymn from the Avesta, Spiegel's Translation, ii. 87.

    8. Hymn from the Avesta, as given by Bunsen in his God in History,' i. 280.

    9. In Augustine's Twenty-three Books Contra Faustum Manichæum,' Faustus is represented as denying that he believes in two gods, but he admits belief in two principles--"Est quidem quod duo principia confitemur."--Lib. 2I. c. I.; Migne's Ed., viii. 387.

    10. Vol. x. p. 177--Milman's Ed.

    11. Autobiography by J. S. Mill, 1873.

    12. "O Mazda! when on earth our spirit is hardly pressed in the fight, come thou to our aid! The pious hearts dost thou give to inherit the earth."--Hymn from the Avesta, as given by Bunsen, i. 280.

    13. Bunsen, i. 317.

    14. Brahma (neut.), Brahmâ (mas.) See [9]Appendix IX.

15. Creuzer's Symbolik, &c., i. 496.
16. Extracts from the Vedanta Philosophy, quoted by Bunsen, i. 332.
17. Ibid.
18. Ibid., 381.
19. Ibid.
20. Extracts from Buddhist Hymns, quoted by Bunsen, i. 346 et seq.
21. Ibid., i. 347.
22. Extracts from Buddhist Hymns, quoted by Bunsen, i. 348.
23. Ibid., p. 353.
24. Burnouf, Int. à l'Hist. du Buddhisme, p. 522.
25. Eccles. ix. 2.

III – OLD TESTAMENT DOCTRINE OF SIN

WHEN we turn from the various systems of Nature-religion, even in their most developed form, to Revelation, we find ourselves in a very different atmosphere. Whence this atmosphere has come--to what special sources we are to trace the higher religious views that here meet us--it is no part of our present business to inquire. This would involve a treatment of the whole subject of Revelation--what it means--how far it is natural, and how far supernatural. It would involve, moreover, the treatment of many literary questions regarding the books of the Old Testament--their age, origin, authenticity, and integrity--all of which we must equally pass by. These are subjects belonging to a different branch of Theology from that with which we are concerned, and they must be dealt with on their own merits. No one in a time like ours, speaking from a scientific point of view, can assume such questions to be settled. While we decline to enter upon them, therefore, we do not venture to assume the conclusions of one school or another regarding them. The dogmatic theologian is not bound to do so. He takes the Bible as he finds it. Whatever may be the authorship and age of its several books, he sees with sufficient clearness that they contain a progressive development of religious thought and sentiment; and he has no difficulty in detecting what general elements of this thought and sentiment are of earlier and what of later origin. No one can doubt, for example--whatever conclusion may be ultimately reached as to the origin and composition of the Pentateuch--that the five books traditionally attributed to Moses contain the earliest Scriptures, and consequently the earliest religious ideas, of the Hebrews. They may or may not also contain later elements. The legal and priestly institutions which they describe may--some of them at least--belong to a period subsequent to that of Moses. But no one who has any historic sense can doubt that the narrative pictures of Genesis belong to a more primitive type of thought than anything else in the Old Testament, and the theologian whose province it is to trace the evolution of Doctrine in Scripture is therefore warranted in assuming them as the starting-point of his exposition. Even if there be the traces here and there of later colouring--of light reflected backwards from a prophetic vision which did not reach its fulness till long after the time of Moses--this would not affect his conclusions. Here and everywhere he must gather together the threads of revealed thought, and discriminate its lines of advance with the best skill he can. No traditionary conception of Revelation or of the contents of Scripture, however hard and fast that conception may be, can save him from this task of interpretation, and help him in the discharge of it. The sum of revealed truth is to him still only what he finds in Scripture.

Our present concern is with the development of the idea of sin in Old Testament Revelation; and our statement is, that so soon as we come within the sphere of this Revelation we find ourselves breathing a different atmosphere from that which comes from any of the Nature-religions of which we have been speaking. In all of these the idea of evil is in some form or another an external idea. It comes to man even in its moral guise--in Zoroastrianism and Hellenism--from the outside. It is a power which holds him--the shadow of destructive Nature-force--or the idealisation of the more complex elements of wrong that surround him in life and society. It is hardly, if at all, an error of his own mind, or the depravation of his own will. But these, on the other hand, are the aspects in which from the first the idea of evil comes before us in Scripture. The spectre arises from within and not from without. The enemy is in man himself, and not in nature or in any symbol drawn from the suggestions of nature or of external life. In other words, as soon as we come within the' sphere of Revelation we have left nature far behind, and are in front of a human Will. The sphere of Revelation is from the beginning the sphere of Morality, towards which we have been slowly rising in our upward advance along the line of Nature-religion.

It is impossible not to be struck with this change, not merely as it affects man, but as it affects nature. Nature is no longer a manifestation of evil powers, or of powers partly evil and partly good. The primitive man of Hebrew literature is placed in a garden eastward in Eden in which there "grows every tree that is pleasant to the sight and good for food." "Every herb which is upon the face of all the earth," and "every tree," and "the fowl of the air," and "every living thing that moveth upon the earth," are all given into the possession of man for rule and enjoyment. Nothing can be further from the picture than any shadow of evil influence. "And God saw everything that He had made, and, behold, it was very good." [26] Man is planted in the midst of these as lord of all. There is no suggestion of conflict--of the struggle of good against evil. There is no evil as yet in nature or in man.

It is impossible to conceive a greater contrast to the picture presented to us in the dawn of the

John Tulloch, D.D.

religious consciousness outside of Revelation. And yet this is only one point of the contrast. There are others still more important. Not only are nature and man set in a different light, but the Divine is, above all, differently conceived. The God or Gods of nature are dual or manifold in their conception--the wavering reflection of man's varying experience of joy and suffering. Their relation to man varies with the promptings of his own heart, and the monitions of his intellect feebly groping to comprehend the problem of his being. In the Hebrew Scriptures the Divine power is drawn from the first with a firm and clear hand, as the creative Source of all being, order, and life. "In the beginning God created the heaven and the earth;" "and God said, Let there be light: and there was light. And God saw the light, that it was good: and God divided the light from the darkness. And God called the light Day, and the darkness He called Night." [27]

It is hardly possible for language to measure the length and breadth of advance which is here represented, beyond any stage of religious thought that is external to the Scriptures. The great features of nature--the heaven and the earth, the light and the darkness--are no longer first, but second. A creative Mind whose word is law stands at their head. A free Will whose work is Providence calls them into being and directs all their movements. Instead of looking with a confused and troubled glance upon the dim personalities of man's imagination in the earth and sky, the sunshine and storm, here we look beyond heaven and earth alike, directly into a region of Divine Intelligence and creative Will. And this fundamental difference makes everything else different. We are no longer in a region of Nature-shadows, but of moral realities,--a Divine Will on one side, and an ordered nature and human will on the other side. And it is out of these essential and primary relations of being that the conception of sin arises. It is a conception which includes evil, and yet is deeper far than any conception of evil we have yet reached.

This will fully appear as we proceed with our exposition,--1st, Of the Fall, or primal act of sin, depicted in the third chapter of Genesis; 2d, Of the several expressions used throughout the Old Testament Scriptures to denote sin; and 3d, and more particularly, as we glance rapidly at the development of the idea in these Scriptures in its relations to the divine law, the divine personality, and the community and mankind at large.

What is known as the Fall, or primal act of sin, not merely stands, after the act of creation, at the fountain-Head of Hebrew literature, but enters more or less into all the developements of the Hebrew religious consciousness. Certain features of the narrative, on the most traditionary view that may be taken of it, are obviously figurative. They are features, that is to say, of a moral incident; and the incident remains the same whether we conceive these features to represent external facts or not. This applies especially to the supposed action and speech of the serpent, and the virtues attributed to "the tree of the knowledge of good and evil." Nothing but confusion of thought can arise from attempting to fix a definite meaning on such accessories of the incident, [28] all the genuine meaning of which arises from the moral portrait which it sets before us. This moral portrait is a true expression of the religious thought of the Hebrews, and it is their thought as to sin which we are in search of, and with which we have now to deal, whatever may be made of the literary vesture or form in which that thought is expressed. Here, as elsewhere, the reality of the thought is not dependent upon the view we may take of the narrative forms in which it is conveyed.

What, then, is the sum of the moral portrait presented to us in the third chapter of Genesis? What are the elements of the primitive religious consciousness of the Hebrews on the subject, as here depicted? There is, first, the reality of a divine will and of a human will in the face of it. The human is the image or reflection of the Divine: "And God said, Let us make man in our image, after our likeness." It is true that this is a part of the prior creation narrative, and not of the Fall narrative, and that these narratives are possibly not from the same original source;--so modern criticism assures us. [See [10]Appendix X.] But whether from diverse sources or not, it is the same thought they reveal. The man who is tempted in the third chapter, is the same man, made in the image of God, spoken of in the first. He is a being, that is to say, gifted with reason and moral freedom; the image and the subject of God. The command given him in the second chapter, which is admitted to belong to the same narrative as the third, is an expression of this subjection, and, at the same time, of man's responsibility. "And the Lord God commanded the man, saying, Of every tree of the garden thou mayest freely eat; but of the tree of the knowledge of good and evil, thou shalt not eat of it: for in the day that thou eatest thereof thou shalt surely die."

This command is presupposed in the third chapter, and forms the key to its whole meaning. Here, therefore, we have two great moral conceptions--conceptions so vital that they lie at the foundation of all Scriptural theology and all Scriptural ethics--the divine will addressing the human will and intelligence which it has called into being; in other words, drawing out still more fully the moral picture presented to us. We have (1) the divine will, (2) the expression of this will in a divine command or law, and (3) a creaturely will the subject of the law; and if all this has as yet nothing to do with sin, it is nevertheless the essential background to the idea. It enables us, and compels us from the first, to set the idea in its true light, and to recognize that its genuine and exclusive meaning is moral, and that it vanishes save in front of the Divine as will and law.

The human will thus placed under authority, and made the subject of a revealed command, is first enticed and then yields to disobedience., "Now the serpent was more subtil than any beast of the field which the Lord God" (Jahveh-Elohim) "had made. And he said unto the woman, Yea, hath God said, Ye shall not eat of every tree of the garden? And the woman said unto the serpent, We may eat of the fruit of the trees of the garden: but of the fruit of the tree which is in the midst of the garden, God hath said, Ye shall not eat of it, neither shall ye touch it, lest ye die. And the serpent said unto the woman, Ye shall not surely die: for God doth know that in the day ye eat thereof, then your eyes shall be opened, and ye shall be as gods, knowing good and evil. And when the woman saw that the tree was good for food, and that it was pleasant to the eyes, and a tree to be desired to make one wise, she took of the fruit thereof, and did eat, and gave also unto her husband with her; and he did eat. And the eyes of them both were opened, and they knew that they were naked." [29] And when they heard the voice of the Lord God in the garden, they were afraid, and hid themselves.

Such is the picture of the Fall. It is unnecessary, and would be quite useless, to try to give any explanation of its special features;--of the serpent; of the form of temptation, and its special nature-- whether ambition or sensuality; of the growth of sinful desire in the woman, her act of disobedience, and the participation of her husband in it; of its effects in the awaking of hitherto unknown conditions of shame in relation to one another and the divine voice. All these aspects of the subject may furnish matters of comment, although I hardly think of reasonable or useful comment, to those who care to inquire into them. But it is not at all necessary to deal specially with them in order to enter into the full meaning of the incident as a moral transaction. The sum of this meaning is plainly that the human will, in face of the divine command, yields to the force of temptation and external inducement, and violates the command. This is the entrance of sin into the world--the transgression of the divine law. The will which was made subject to law--the happiness of which was to lie within the law, in obedience to it-- turns against it and seeks its happiness outside of the law, in opposition to it. The revolt, moreover, is induced by external enticement or influence; in other words, the will or spirit becomes subject to evil suggestion and the influence of Nature in place of divine law. This is the moral essence of the story. Let us draw out more fully its several points. They sum up a world of meaning, which no analysis can well exhaust.

(a.) Evil, as it emerges upon us in the primitive Hebrew consciousness, is not something outside of us, but essentially something in us. It is the wilful turning away from the Divine, clearly revealed, expressing itself clearly and unequivocally in conscience--"Ye shall not eat of it, neither shall ye touch it, lest ye die;" and the wilful yielding to Nature or some outside influence--"As good for food, pleasant to the eyes, or to be desired to make one wise." It is this that makes the evil. The outside--Nature--has only force or power over the will after it has yielded from within to it. Or at least, the will must turn from the Divine to something else not Divine, before the evil lays hold of it. Something else must be desirable in preference before the evil emerges. In other words, the good lies in the conformity of the divine and human will. The evil can only arise from their nonconformity.

But it may be said, Is the evil not already posited outside of man in the idea of the serpent as the tempter? Have we not here the evil Power already opposed to the good, and man represented as his victim snatched by his wiles from the possession and enjoyment of the good? The later thought of Jewish theology and the Christian Church, in its various branches, have associated the evil personality known as Satan or the Devil with the serpent of Genesis. And good reasons may be urged for this association. The idea of the serpent tempting man and exciting him to evil, points to the idea of an evil Principle having already entered into the world and acquired influence in it. The cunning with which the serpent works upon the desire of the woman to rise above the limits of her creaturely existence, and be as God to whom she is rightfully subject, is truly diabolical. No doubt, therefore, was felt on this point in the later Jewish Church; and the Christian consciousness, which was influenced so largely by Jewish thought, readily took up the idea and expanded it. But in the narrative of Genesis, taken by itself, there is nothing of this later view. The serpent is more subtil than any beast of the field, but nothing more. The curse pronounced against him alludes entirely to his animal nature. And as a mere matter of historical criticism, therefore, we are not warranted in transferring the later conception to the earlier stage of Hebrew thought. Whatever we may make of the serpent and his cunning, we cannot say that a Power, and still less a Spirit, of evil was already conceived by the Hebrew mind as clearly existing outside of man. I do not profess to explain fully this feature of the incident. I am content to leave many things unexplained in Scripture and elsewhere. Possibly there were elements in the Hebrew consciousness, with all its moral elevation, which clung to an outside view of evil or the association of evil influence with certain aspects or animals of nature. It would be strange, indeed, if there were not survivals of the old Nature-worship of the Chaldean tribes, out of which Abraham came, among his descendants. All that it is necessary to say here is, that in the narrative of the Fall, taken by itself, there is no suggestion of a distinct Power of Evil--like that which is found in Zoroastrianism--having a share in man no less than the good power. Man is not made evil because there is evil already without him, from which he cannot escape. He is made evil because he yields from within to the gratification of lawless desire externally excited. The object of desire is before him. An evil voice whispers to him that the evil is good, and the good evil. He listens, yields, and falls under the voice of temptation and the prompting of his own desire. But the very fact of desire beyond the law is already sin, and without this desire the evil would never have laid hold of him. The essential evil does not, therefore, come to him from without, but from within. Man makes himself a sinner.

(b) Not only so. Evil, as conceived by the Hebrew religious consciousness, is not only from within, a revolt of the self-will from the divine will, but it is a self-rejection of an order which is felt to be wise and good. It is a fall from an ideal acknowledged to be divine. "But of the fruit of the tree which is in the midst of the garden, God hath said, Ye shall not eat of it, neither shall ye touch it, lest ye die." This is the acknowledgment of the woman. She has no doubt of the divine order., It is the way at once of wisdom and of pleasantness. The voice of God utters itself unmistakably in the heart; but the desire of the eyes, the pleasantness of the outside, of the tree fair and beautiful, and apparently "good for food," prevails, and the sinful act is consummated. Paradise is lost; the ideal approven by the higher nature vanishes, never to be recalled. The knowledge of good and evil is indeed gained, but at a price which brings with it only shame and confusion of face.

Nothing can be further from the Biblical conception than any idea of evil entering into humanity as a necessary factor in its development. The Fall is truly a stumble--in no sense a step in advance. It may be that compensation is to be found in it at last, and that the knowledge of the evil as well as the good was necessary to carry man forward beyond the childlike naivete of the paradisiacal state, in which he dwelt in harmony with the Divine above him and nature around him. The world of human intelligence, industry, and art, as we know it, may be inconceivable in connection with the primitive man. Evil may all along have been as necessary to its development as good. The very idea of progress may posit the evil as a necessary condition. This may be all true: all we say is, that there is no countenance given to such a view in the Biblical picture. The suggestion of a higher knowledge as the result of disobedience comes from the tempter. It lies within the temptation itself as its most powerful spring,--that the intellectual nature of the man and woman were to be advanced by the act of self-assertion; and the fact of this advance is so far acknowledged from the divine side. [30] Man is allowed to have gained in intellect, and so far to have come nearer the Divine ("like one of us") by the knowledge of evil. But his intellectual gain is his moral loss. The suggestion of the tempter is not the less a lie because there happened in it to be a side of truth. It was the bait of a richer being--of a higher happiness--that he had held before the woman. The bait was not altogether deceptive. The being is enlarged by the mental experience of evil, but it loses far more than it gains. It loses cheerful communion with the Divine; it loses the sense of self-approval; it is driven forth from Paradise. Adam and Eve have grown at once to the consciousness of manhood and womanhood--they are no longer as children in a garden--but they are at the same time ashamed of one another, and afraid of God. In short, they have fallen; they have lost a sure position--they have gained an uncertain future. The idea of a fall, of a distinct moral loss not to be recovered, is carefully and completely preserved; and whatever later theory may have made of a balance even of moral good in the origin of evil, there is nothing to encourage such a theory in the early picture. From the moral side--and this is the essential side--the picture is dark throughout.

(c.) All this is more clearly evident from the idea of death associated with the picture. The divine prohibition, as to the "fruit of the tree in the midst of the garden," was, "Ye shall not eat of it, neither shall ye touch it, lest ye die." The suggestion of the tempter was, "Ye shall not surely die;" [31] and, finally, the man is driven from the garden, lest he "take also of the tree of life, and eat, and live for ever." [32] Out of these well-known features of the story has come the intimate association of death with the Fall--an association frequently repeated in Scripture, and which will come before us for special consideration in the writings of St. Paul. All that is necessary to say now is that, whatever more general interpretation we may put upon these intimations, they must be supposed chiefly to point to the moral loss or injury involved in the act of disobedience. Death, as a simple physical fact, is unaffected by moral conditions. Its character may be greatly altered, and no doubt has been greatly altered, by the fact of sin; but its incidence is natural, and lies in the constitution of things. There is nothing in the passage which makes us think otherwise. Death is intimated as the hazard of disobedience, and the idea of perpetuated existence is connected with the eating of the tree of life. Theologians have pictured the glories of an unfallen state, and the immortality of a sinless race; but there is nothing in the Biblical text to warrant such pictures. It is nowhere indicated that man would have been immortal in Eden if he had not sinned. Physical dissolution did not directly follow the act of sin, and is not connected with it as immediate cause and effect. What is really always connected with sin is the destruction of the higher nature or self, which loses strength and dies under the power of evil when once accepted. In the very moment of sin it receives this death into itself, [33] for it thereby passes out of the condition of spiritual healthfulness, and, in falling below the fulness of the divine life which belongs to it, may be said to die. Sin is, therefore, not only the loss of an ideal which man might have enjoyed, but it is an element of death working destruction in the fallen will which has yielded to it, if not immediately, yet not the less surely. This was the true loss or penalty incurred by Adam; and here, as elsewhere, we are to look for a spiritual and not a literal meaning in the narrative. To do otherwise is merely to entangle ourselves in hopeless difficulties.

2. Such are the main features of the Fall, and the same moral features appear more or less plainly in the expressions used to denote sin in the Old Testament. There is a considerable variety of such expressions, but it cannot be said that any clear ethical progress is marked by their use. They occur, if not indiscriminately, yet without marking any definite advance from period to period of Hebrew thought. Some, however, are more general, and others more particular; and it may be well to begin with the more general, which at the same time are more frequent in occurrence.

(a.) The most frequent and universal word for sin in the Old Testament is chatath, [34] from a verb which originally signifies, exactly like its Greek representative in the New Testament, to miss the mark.[35] It is used in its primary physical meaning in the Book of Judges,[36] where men are spoken of as being each able to sling stones at an hair's-breadth "and not miss." Chatath is the term used in the seventh verse of the fourth chapter of Genesis, where the expression "sin" first occurs in our English version, in reference to the sacrifice of Cain. Sometimes in our version it is rendered more precisely fault,[37] sometimes trespass,[38] sometimes harm,[39] and blame.[40] The idea conveyed in the expression is one of the most rudimentary as well as comprehensive in relation to sin--the idea of failure. Whatever sin may otherwise be, it is always failure,--a departure from the straight road--a missing of the point aimed at, or which should have been aimed at. The idea of right, and not merely of success, is implied as the correlative of the expression. There is a right--an aim which it is not merely an advantage to have achieved, but which ought to be achieved. And to miss this aim is not merely to fail in the sense of deficiency, but it is to go out of the right way and make a mistake. Man was made for the right, and every departure from it is a departure from the true purpose for which he was made. And this is the fundamental and universal idea of sin conveyed in Scripture.

(b.) The expression avon [41] is commonly taken as denoting the next most characteristic definition of sin. The original meaning is crookedness, perversity, from a verb [42] "to bend," "distort," or "turn out of the right course." The same rudimentary idea, therefore, is so far conveyed here as in the previous expression. As there is a right mark or point to be aimed at, so there is always a right line towards it. And sin is not only failure as missing the mark, but perversity as taking a wrong line. The divine life springing from its fountain-head is not only the creative, but is designed to be also the directive principle, both of humanity and the world; and sin arises whenever the course of this life is turned aside and deflected. There seems a deeper moral meaning, therefore, in this expression--the idea not only of failure which might arise from mere deficiency and lack of strength, but of intentional wrongness. And, upon the whole, the use of the expression bears out this deeper meaning. It is the expression applied by Cain to his own sin, when he has heard the curse pronounced against him, and begins to realise its true magnitude.[43] It is the word also used by Judah when he and his brethren stand before Joseph arraigned for having carried away his cup, which had been found in Benjamin's sack. "And Judah said, What shall we speak? or how shall we clear ourselves? God hath found out the iniquity of thy servants." [44] It is still more significantly used in the Psalms--as, for example, in the thirty-second and fifty-first Psalms, both of which are indeed storehouses of all the main expressions denoting sin. "Blessed is he whose transgression" (pesha) "is forgiven, whose sin" (chätaah) "is covered. Blessed is the man unto whom the Lord imputeth not iniquity" (avon). "I acknowledged my sin" (cattathi) "unto Thee, and mine iniquity" (avoni) "have I not hid. I said, I will confess my transgressions" (peshaai) "unto the Lord; and Thou forgavest the iniquity of my sin" (avon chattathi).[45] Again: "Wash me thoroughly from mine iniquity" (avoni), "and cleanse me from my sin" (chattathi). "For I acknowledge my transgressions" (peshaai): "and my sin" (chattathi) "is ever before me. Against Thee, Thee only, have I sinned" (the ordinary verb chata), "and done this evil" (ra) "in thy sight. . . Behold, I was shapen in iniquity" (avon); "and in sin" (chet) [46] "did my mother conceive me." [47]

It is unnecessary to enter into further details, or to press any additional force that may seem to be in this expression. It would be too much to say that it is always discriminated from the former word by a precise shade of meaning--as, for example, in the last words quoted from the Psalmist's confession of sin. We nowhere find in the language of moral experience such precise adjustments of meaning--no more in Hebrew or Greek than in our own language. On the contrary, the expressions have a tendency to pass into one another, and to become mixed in their application, just as the words "sin" and "iniquity" with us. The former, however, remains the more general, the latter the more special expression. And it is the same with the Hebrew equivalents. The idea of wrongness in fact--failure, missing the mark--and the idea of wrongness in intention--injustice, iniquity--are the ideas respectively conveyed. And this reference to the will implied in the last word gives it a deeper shade of meaning. It brings out more prominently the moral character of the act, and fixes it home upon the sinner. And hence the word passes naturally into the idea of "guilt," for which it is often used in the earlier Scriptures; as in the expressions, "The iniquity" or guilt "of the Amorites is not yet full;" [48] "Visiting the iniquity" or guilt "of the fathers upon . . . the third generation;" [49] and again, in a passage where we have, as in the passage quoted from the Psalms, all the three expressions close together. "Forgiving iniquity" (guilt), and "transgression and sin." [50]

(c.) There is another word, aven, [51] which is very often translated in our version "iniquity," [52] but which primarily means "vanity" and "nothingness." [53] As applied to our subject, it seems to convey the idea of the unreality or nothingness of all evil or opposition to the Divine. Powerful or successful as it may seem for a time, it must prove in the end unprofitable and vain.

(d.) But a more important word is that which we have already found so often associated both with chattah and avon--viz., pesha, [54] which our translators have generally rendered transgression, sometimes trespass, [55] sometimes rebellion. [56] These renderings as nearly as possible convey the meaning of the word, which seems always to imply as its background the idea of a divine law, which has been broken or transgressed. There is here, therefore, also a strongly personal or moral meaning. All sorts of sins, acts of weakness, negligence, or carelessness, are implied in the primary expression chattah; but sins of design and violent purpose are specially implied by pesha. There is no passage brings this out more fully than the one in Job already indicated along with others--a passage which is translated in our version, "For he addeth rebellion" (pesha) ("unto his sin" (chattatho).

(e.) In addition to these words, there are the general expression ra, [57] denoting evil in all senses, physical, ethical, and accidental, [58] and resha, [59] commonly rendered wickedness, from a root to make a noise or tumult. This term is supposed to express the disposition of evil--evil become a habit--or the quality of unrighteousness, just as tzedek [60] is the quality of righteousness.

(f.) There is still a further word which claims attention before we close this analysis--viz., asham, [61] generally translated in our version as trespass or guilt, and carefully discriminated from chattath in its application to the Mosaic sacrifices; the one denoting the sin-offering, and the other the trespass-offering. Asham is derived from a root (asham) which means to fail, having for "its primary idea negligence, especially in going or gait." (Gesen.) It seems to have everywhere a more special meaning than chattath, as indeed all the other words we have been considering have. The specialty in this case seems to point to definite acts of sin, violations of law and commandment which have been brought home to the offender or offenders--for example, in the forty-second chapter of the Book of Genesis, [62] where we have one of the first and most typical uses of the word. It is when the offence committed against Joseph flashes suddenly on the minds of his brethren, under the force of his demand to bring Benjamin into Egypt, that they say one to another, "We are verily guilty" (ashemin) "concerning our brother." Frequently the word is used in reference to public sins, as when the numbering of the people is spoken of in the First Book of Chronicles [63] as a cause of trespass (asham) to Israel; and still more frequently for sin, either ignorant or wilful, against definite prohibitions of the law. [64] In the sixty-ninth Psalm [65] it is used to denote particular acts of sin: "O God, Thou knowest my foolishness; and my sins are not hid from Thee."

It is unnecessary to dwell further upon these details,-the chief interest of which consists in the various and dispersing light which they throw around the idea of sin. v All of them from the most general to the most particular, imply a moral significance; in other words, they connect the idea of sin with a human personality--some of them more closely than others, but all of them more or less. To "miss a mark," "to deviate from the straight road," "to break some rule or law," all involve definitely the action of an intelligent will, which not only might have done otherwise, but which ought to have done otherwise. In some cases the mistake, deviation, or transgression may not have been of purpose, but rather the result of weakness, negligence, or carelessness. But in no case is it suggested that the sinful act was inevitable or necessary, or, in other words, that the evil coming forth in human actions was beyond man's control, or a mere part of his nature wielded from without. In most cases the act is expressly referred to the free will or personality of the actor, and condemned as such. A moral meaning in the act is therefore everywhere asserted.

3. When we turn finally to view the subject under the successive phases of the Old Testament religion, this character of sin still more clearly appears. It everywhere comes forth as an act of the human will done against the divine will, or some special institutions supposed to represent the divine will. Sometimes the sinful act is more prominently held forth in relation to God as Supreme Creator and Governor, as Head of the world, and the Lord and Sovereign of men. This is the pervading idea of Genesis. "And the Lord said, My spirit shall not always strive with man. . . . And God saw that the wickedness" (ra) "of man was great in the earth, and that every imagination of the thoughts of his heart was only evil" (ra) "continually." [66] In such statements as these, and generally throughout the earlier portions of the divine Revelation, the conception of sin is more objective and general. It is something wrong in the disposition or state of man towards the Divine, something always for which man is responsible. But there is no analysis of the conception, beyond the fact that it is at variance with the divine order.

As we advance beyond the simple imaginations of the Patriarchal to the more elaborate culture of the Mosaic times, the conception both deepens in moral significance and acquires a more varied emphasis. If we are allowed to bring into view the ample machinery of the so-called Mosaic legislation,

The Christian Doctrine of Sin

it is needless to point out how greatly the idea of sin must have become enlarged, or at least widened, in the face of that legislation. The different orders of sacrifice, and the minutiae of the ceremonial and social laws of the Hebrews, all point to special kinds of sin, called into vivid recognition by the theocratic restrictions everywhere encompassing the chosen people. An authoritative divine ritual touching the national life at every point necessarily diffused a widespread sense of obligation, which too frequently remained unfulfilled. A danger, it is true, lay in this very diffusion, illustrated by the Hebrew history as by all sacerdotal history. The numerous Levitical ordinances had a tendency to draw the sense of sin towards the surface, and so far to empty it of moral meaning--a result more or less seen in every species of sacerdotalism. When men are led to concentrate religious attention upon external acts, they begin to lose something of inward depth and spiritual reality; and religion often perishes in the very multitude of religious forms. The history of the Jewish religion is certainly no exception to this rule.

Should we not feel warranted in attributing all the ceremonial and sacerdotal legislation of the Pentateuch to the time of Moses, Mosaism yet remains a great institution, powerful in moral influence. The ten "words" or commandments which even the most advanced criticism carries up to Moses, are in literature the most profound and comprehensive expression of that great order which encompasses all moral life. The moral law powerfully contributed to awaken the inner sense of the Hebrew people, and deepen their consciousness of sin. The Divine is presented in it not merely as Sovereign and Lord--although this is the opening key-note [67] --but as identified with every aspect of order, truth, righteousness, and purity in human life, A moral ideal not only invests all life, but is carried up to Jahveh-Elohim as the Source of this life and its highest Exemplar. It was impossible to dwell in the light of such an ideal and not to have had the spiritual sense quickened and made sensitive, and the feeling of offence towards the Divine called forth in many ways hitherto little understood or owned. This is what St. Paul means when he says that "the law entered that the offence might abound;" [68] and again, that "without the law sin was dead." [69] He is speaking of his own experience, or of the experience of a devout Jew in his own time; but the experience of the religious nature is always so far the same--nay, the experience of the individual is typical of the race. When the law entered into the consciousness of Humanity, and was added to the progressive force of divine Revelation, the sense of sin was deepened alongside of it. Conscience became alive in front of the divine commandment, and spiritual life was touched to its depths by that sad undertone of sin which has never died out of it. Through ages, the moral law has been the most powerful moral factor of humanity, restraining its chaotic tendencies, and binding it into harmonies of domestic, social, and religious well-being. It has lain not merely upon the human conscience, but entered into the human heart as one of its most living inward springs-bracing its weakness, rebuking its laxity, holding before it an inflexible rule of moral good. Words cannot measure the strength which it has been to all the higher qualities of the race, and the widespread moral education which it has diffused--discriminating and purifying the ideas alike of good and evil wherever it has prevailed, and clothing life with a reality and depth of meaning which it would never otherwise have possessed.

With the development of Hebrew thought in the prophetic writings and the Psalms, all the special characteristics of sin come out yet more prominently. The prophetic order in its highest signification was nothing else than a living witness for those eternal principles of righteousness which previous Revelation had implanted in the Hebrew race, and through them in the life of Humanity. The prophets were the preachers of that holy religion of Jahveh which, beginning with Abraham, instituted by Moses, and consolidated by David and Solomon, runs through Hebrew history with all its vacillations and reversions as a golden thread, making it a power of spiritual elevation and blessing for the world. Continually, when the national consciousness of the Divine sank or became perverted, it was revived, reinforced, and once more turned in a right direction. The reality of the divine government under which Israel lived, of the exclusive claims of the worship of Jahveh, and of the essential antagonism betwixt this worship and all deeds of sinful disorder and impurity, was once more awakened and brought into the clear light of national recognition. This was the work of the prophets more than all others.: It was they who kept alive the moral thoughtfulness of the chosen people. The priestly sacrifices and ordinances, valuable as they were, were apt, like all forms of ritual, to degenerate into formalities. In themselves, they were not and could not be sources of spiritual good--it was only the divine feeling which lay behind their use which gave them any religious value; and when this feeling failed, they helped to choke it up and externalise it rather than to call it forth afresh. The law was a constant monition of divine duty; but, as the frequent lapses into idolatry prove, its very first word was too often forgotten and powerless. Neither the priestly nor the moral side of Mosaism, it may be said, could have preserved in any purity the religious thought of Hebraism, surrounded as it was by so many depressing influences, to which it was continually yielding. It required a distinct force to renovate and recruit it from time to time. And this it found in prophecy, which for more than six hundred years was its most powerful element of religious revival, and remains to this day the most vital factor of Hebrew literature.[See [11]Appendix XI.]

With this continual revival of divine consciousness in the Hebrew people the consciousness of sin revived, deepened, and became more real. It was felt as an offence not merely against divine law or precept, but against a Divine Person, a living One who had claims upon the life of all His servants, and the violation of whose commandments was disobedience of His will. The prophet was always the messenger of God. The word of God came unto him, and he could not but utter it. He was not only the preacher of the law and its righteous demands, but he was the direct organ of the divine voice and will; and through him the sense of a supreme personal authority, whom it was sin to disobey, was brought near to the Hebrew mind. There cannot be a better illustration of this than the fifty-first Psalm, which represents the results of the dealing of the prophet Nathan with David in the matter of Bathsheba. An act of definite transgression is not only brought home to the conscience of the king, but conscience is quickened throughout, and the divine presence made so living to it that every other aspect of the king's conduct disappears in the overwhelming sense that it was sin--against the law, indeed, but above all against the author of the law--against God Himself. "For I acknowledge my transgressions: and my sin is ever before me. Against Thee, Thee only, have I sinned, and done this evil in Thy sight; that Thou mightest be justified when Thou speakest, and be clear when Thou judgest. Behold, I was shapen in iniquity; and in sin did my mother conceive me." [70] There is no more comprehensive or individual expression of sin in all the Old Testament Scriptures. It is a definite act of transgression or violation of law; it is a consciousness of guilt ever before the awakened soul; it is, more than all, a consciousness of offence against God, who has given the law, and who has endowed the soul with the capacity of serving Him. Withal it is the outcome of an evil nature. Sin is personal, and the sinner without excuse. Yet its origin lies beyond the individual will. It is an inheritance of nature which comes to us with our birth. All these aspects of the subject are presented in the verses I have quoted, which occur irresistibly to the student of Scripture in speaking of it. There is no thought of definition. The different sides of the subject are not put forward in any systematic relation to one another. They come forth only as the cries of a manifold experience which knows and thinks of nothing but the burden which it bears. And so the same experience repeats itself--if not in the same comprehensive manner--in many an utterance of Psalm and prophecy. Wherever the voice of the prophet was heard sounding the depth of the souls that he addressed, there was the response of repentance and confession: "I acknowledge my transgression." "Against Thee, Thee only, have I sinned." The fact of divine law came near to the sinner; the fact of the divine presence overwhelmed him. The thought of God evoked the consciousness of sin, and drove it home upon the sinner's heart.

The same word of prophecy brought out more distinctly than before the universality of sin, and its persistence in the nation and the world. The prophet was a preacher of righteousness to the individual conscience. But he was even more a national preacher and reformer. He put himself forward as a public man, and dealt with all the aspects of public life. He was, as has been said, [71] "a power in the nation," and all the elements of national life are graphically depicted in his pages. It is impossible to peruse these pages without recognising how pervading a presence evil is everywhere felt to be. It is a state and quality diffused throughout the nation--a characteristic of humanity. While originating in individual self-will, it is not merely the result of will in every particular case, but has so permeated the mass of human nature, that its thoughts are evil, and only evil. This conception of pervasive influence of sin goes back, indeed, to the very opening of Revelation, as shown in the words of Genesis already quoted[72] regarding the Flood. It is of the nature of sin to multiply and diffuse its power, repeating itself by example and a degraded tone of general feeling. And pervading as its influence, are its fatal consequences. Like a subtle poison, it not only contaminates and injures the individual, but the family, the tribe, the race. It kills wherever it spreads. Its original penalty is an inherent penalty. It works death by its own direct action, cutting off the life of man from God--the only source of life--and leaving behind only a perverted and self-destroying image of human activity.

As a whole, we may sum up the doctrine of the Old Testament as follows, gathering into one view the results of our analysis:--

(1.) The Hebrew conception of evil is distinctively moral. It is the disobedience of the human will against the Divine expressed in the form of command, revelation, or law. In other words, it is what we specially mean by sin.

(2.) It is not only a violation of divine law, but a rejection of divine good.

(3.) All sin is in its nature destructive. It bears death in it as its natural working or outcome.

(4.) It is not merely individual, but diffusive. Having once entered into human nature, it becomes a part of it, an hereditary taint, passing from generation to generation, often with accelerated force.

(5.) It is connected with a power or powers of evil outside of man, the character and influence of which are as yet but dimly revealed.

(6.) And to these several points of our summary we may add a further, which has been emphasised by certain expositors of the religion of Israel. Evil is also connected with the will of Jahveh as the supreme source of all energy and all events. Facts of evil (ra), no less than of good, are traced upwards to the Almighty Will, as the ultimate source of all things. [73] This is true beyond all question; but it exceeds the truth to say, as Kuenen does, [74] that the older Israelitish prophets and historians did not

The Christian Doctrine of Sin

hesitate to derive even moral evil from Jahveh. Precise distinctions of morality and contingency were unfamiliar to the Hebrew mind; and at no time would this mind have shrunk from attributing every form of evil accident (however immediately caused by human wickedness) to the Sovereign Power, which did as it willed in heaven and on earth. But it is nevertheless true, as has been clearly seen in the course of our exposition, that the essential idea of evil in the Hebrew mind was so far from associating itself with the Divine Will, that its special note or characteristic was opposition to this Will. The line of later argument, as to a possible relation of the Divine Will to sin (whereby its omnipotence and yet its purity should be preserved), is foreign to the Old Testament. It grasps events concretely; it does not analyse them in their origin or nature; and so, while it hesitates not to ascribe all evil as matter of fact, and as part of the universal providence which governs the world, to the Divine Will, it never fails to set forth sin as springing out of the depths of human personality in opposition to the Divine. This idea is stamped on every page of the Old Testament, and no concrete figures of prophetic rhetoric can be allowed to efface so clear and deep an impression.

Footnotes:
26. Gen. i. 31.
27. Gen. i. 1, 3-5.
28. This was clearly pointed out long ago in Dr. Hill's Lectures--to refer to a well-known Scotch theological authority--vol. ii. p. 4, 5, "Several parts of the history," he says, "cannot be understood in a literal sense. Thus it is not to be supposed that the tree of which man was forbidden to eat had the power which the name seems to imply, and which the serpent suggests, of making those who ate the fruit wise, knowing good and evil; neither is it to be supposed that the serpent at that time possessed those powers of speech and reason which the narrative seems to ascribe to him, or that the plain meaning of the words, 'The seed of the woman shall bruise the head of the serpent,' expresses the whole punishment of the tempter."
29. Gen. iii. 1-7.
30. Gen. iii. 2.
31. Gen. iii. 3, 4.
32. Gen. iii. 22.
33. "The soul that sinneth, it shall die."--Ezek. xviii. 4, 20.
34. cht't
35. Hamartano
36. Judges, xx. 16.
37. Gen. xli. 9; Exod. v. 16.
38. 1 Kings, viii. 31.
39. Levit. v. 16.
40. Gen. xliii. 9.
41. vn
42. vh
43. Gen. iv. 13.
44. Gen. xliv. 16.
45. Psalm xxxii. 1, 2, 5.
46. cht'. This simple form of the word occurs pretty frequently, and the form cht'h occasionally.
47. Psalm li. 2-5.
48. Gen. xv. 16.
49. Exod. xx. 5.
50. vn vphs vcht'h--Exod. xxxiv. 7.
51. 'vn.
52. No fewer than thirty-eight times, it is said.
53. As in such passages as Amos, v. 5, "And Bethel shall come to nought;" and Isaiah, xli. 29, "Behold, they are all vanity; their works are nothing,"--the word is connected with 'yn ,'yn, from an unused root lt., implying the idea of negation. The term is translated in the Septuagint, anomia adikia, and occasionally ponos kopos.
54. phs--Septuagint, asebeia, adikia anomia.
55. Gen. xxxi. 36, l. 17; Exod. xxii. 9; 1 Sam. xxv. 28; Hosea, viii. 1, &c.
56. 1. Kings, xii. 19; Job, xxxiv. 37.
57. r.
58. Levit. xxvii. 10; Gen. viii. 21; Isa. iii. 11.
59. rs.
60. tsdq.
61. 'sm.
62. Gen. xlii. 21.

63. 1 Chron. xxi. 3.
64. Num. v. 6, 7; Levit. vi. 2-7.
65. Ps. lxix. 5.
66. Gen. vi. 3-5.
67. "I am the Lord thy God. . . . Thou shalt have no other gods before me."--Exod. xx. 2, 3.
68. Rom. v. 20.
69. Rom. vii. 8.
70. Psalm li. 3-5.
71. J. S. Mill, Represent. Gov., 4l--passage quoted in Appendix XI.
72. Gen. vi. 5. See p. 86.
73. "I form the light, and create darkness; I make peace, and create evil: I the Lord" (Jahveh) "do all these things,"--Isaiah, xlv, 7. "Shall there be evil in a city, and the Lord" (Jahveh) "hath not done it?"--Amos, iii. 6.
74. Religion of Israel, iii. 40. See [12]Appendix XII.

IV – DOCTRINE OF SIN AS CONTAINED IN THE GOSPELS

IN passing to the Christian revelation and the doctrine of sin laid down in the New Testament Scriptures, we carry with us the same moral atmosphere as in the Old Testament. We are everywhere in the same region of divine law and of personal responsibility. Whatever Christianity may be more than Mosaism and Judaism, it embraces at least all the moral truth which they contained. The spiritual consciousness of righteousness, and of sin as its violation, which has accumulated in the long education of the chosen people, is passed over in its full import to the Christian Church, which, in spiritual experience and organic development, is the direct descendant of the Jewish Church. Much besides enters from the first into Christianity,--a new power of life from above--a new creative force; but it loses nothing of the moral experience which has been growing for ages in the Jewish race. It takes this all up, appropriates, enlarges, and purifies it. In this respect conspicuously Christ came not "to destroy, but to fulfil." Upon this inherited experience of divine law, moral motive, and personal responsibility to a higher will, He took His stand and began His work as a Teacher and a Saviour.

It is this organic connection betwixt the Old and the New Testament, and the moral truths which underlie both and make so much of their substance, which compels the theologian to deal with both spheres of Revelation, and seek for the elucidation of Christian truth not only in the pages of the New Testament, but in the pre-Christian pages of the Old. All who ignore this connection will be found to misconceive one or other of these spheres, and to mistake the unity of the divine plan for the education of our race. The connection will be found to hold more or less in reference to all Christian doctrines, even those which seem at first most removed from the Hebrew consciousness; but in the case of the doctrine with which we are dealing, it holds in a special manner. The Christian doctrine of sin is at least all the doctrine which we have found in the Old Testament. It may contain--it does, as we shall find, contain--more than we have drawn from the latter. There is new and further and higher light thrown upon man's moral condition by the teaching of our Lord and of His apostles. But what we have already reached is also found in their teaching, and forms everywhere its basis, asserted or implied; and hence the necessity of our dwelling, as we did in a separate Lecture, on the Old Testament view of sin. In doing so, we were dealing not merely with necessary preliminary matter, but we had already entered within that continuous line of thought and experience which issues in the full Christian doctrine, and forms such an essential part of it that without it the Christian doctrine cannot be fully comprehended.

In the exposition of the fully-developed doctrine of the New Testament Scriptures, there are at least two main aspects in which we must consider it--viz., first, as presented in our Lord's teaching, as given in the Gospels; and second, as elaborately set forth and explained in the Epistles of St. Paul. I am quite aware that this is an inadequate division or classification of the New Testament writings for general dogmatic purposes. The type of doctrine presented in the fourth Gospel is so separable from that presented in the synoptics,--and the writings of St. John--the Gospels and the Epistles, I mean--stand so obviously by themselves in a more advanced line of thought than all the other writings of the Christian Scriptures,--that their dogmatic meaning demands almost always separate treatment. There may be said to be at least the three following types of thought in the New Testament: (1) The Judæo-Christian, represented by the first two synoptics, the Epistle of James, and, less definitely, the Epistles of St. Peter and Jude; (2) the Pauline, represented, in addition to the Epistles of the great apostle, by the Gospel of St. Luke and the Acts of the Apostles; and (3) the Johannean, represented by the fourth Gospel and the three Epistles of St. John. There are few dogmas of the Christian system upon which this last group, or the writings of St. John, have not a distinctive bearing, or a bearing so special as to demand special notice. But as regards the present subject, this cannot be said to be the case, for the simple reason that the experience of sin was a common inheritance in all the sections of the infant Church. It was nothing new--something, indeed, very old--which they knew as Jews, no less than as Christians. There was nothing, therefore, to make the sin-consciousness different in the different apostles, or to make their mode of representing our Lord's teaching regarding it marked by more than casual diversity. Upon the whole, it is essentially the same picture in this respect that we have in all the four Gospels. There may be distinctions to be noticed, but these distinctions do not affect the substance of the representation. We are warranted, therefore, in taking together all that the Gospels have to say regarding sin; or in viewing

John Tulloch, D.D.

our Lord's teaching on this subject in all the four as one complete picture. The doctrine of St. Paul deserves separate treatment, not as being different from that of the Gospels, but as being so expanded and elaborate that it can only be handled adequately by itself. The great apostle, in consistency with his deeper experience and more varied culture, dwells specially, and at length, upon the subject, and in a critical and explanatory manner quite different from that of the Gospels. He enters not only into an analysis of the fact, but into what may be called its philosophy, and so sets forth a comprehensive doctrine, which has powerfully moulded the thought of the Church in all subsequent ages. Our remaining Lectures will be fully occupied in the consideration of this doctrine.

In approaching the present aspect of our subject, we are met at the outset not only with the accumulated moral experience derived from the Old Testament, but, moreover, with a new or at least more clearly developed background of evil. In the Old Testament, evil appears mainly as an inward or subjective conception. The primal sin, although prompted by evil influence from without, is conspicuously inward and moral; everywhere it is the thoughts of men's hearts or the motions of their will, that are evil and obnoxious to God. It is strange how little is seen of any evil Power outside the human will, or any background of a kingdom of evil moving men from without. The connection of Satan, or the evil Power, with the serpent in the Garden of Eden, is an inference of later dogmatic opinion, arising naturally out of the circumstances and the expressions which are afterwards used in the New Testament regarding "that old serpent, which is the Devil, and Satan;" [75] but not only is there no mention of Satan in the narrative of the Fall, but the name does not occur in all the Pentateuch, or any of the earlier Hebrew Scriptures. The expression is, at the most, only used as a proper name five times in the Old Testament--viz., in the opening of the twenty-first chapter of the First Book of Chronicles; [76] in three well-known places in Job, [77] and in the prophecy of Zechariah, in the opening of the third chapter, where Joshua the high priest is represented as "standing before the angel of the Lord, and Satan standing at his right hand to resist him." In all the other places in which the word occurs, it is used in its simple meaning of "adversary," a sense in which it is also used in the Gospels. [78]

Even the most expressive of these Old Testament passages gives us no definite idea of a spiritual Power of evil outside of man, and subjecting man to his control. In the prologue of the Book of Job, Satan is represented, with sufficient clearness, as a distinct being or personal existence. But the picture of his character and of his employment is neither imposing nor spiritual. He is not a grand or impressive figure. He comes among the "sons of God" to present himself before the Lord. He is the image of restlessness, of malice, and of envy--the willing envoy of inflicting mischief upon Job; but he has no semblance of the "Archangel ruined," nor does he assail the patriarch with spiritual weapons. No power of spiritual injury is ascribed to him. He is a delegated Agent in the hands of God, sent forth by Him to execute His purposes; and the power which he exercises is only a power over outward circumstances.

So soon as we come within the sphere of New Testament Revelation, a very different picture is presented to us. From the first there is here depicted a clear and powerful background of evil--a kingdom of evil spirits or "demons," with a prince or ruler at their head, designated by various names, as "the Devil," "the Tempter," [79] "Satan," [80] "Beelzebub," [81] "the Prince of Devils," [82] "the Strong One," [83] "the Wicked One," [84] "the Enemy," or "the Hostile One." [85] The first three epithets are all used in what may be called the primitive account of our Lord's temptation, in the fourth chapter of St. Matthew's Gospel; and throughout the Gospels the words "Satan," "the Devil," "the Wicked One," "Beelzebub," "the Prince of Devils" (or, as the translation ought to have been here, as elsewhere, "Demons"), are used interchangeably. There can be no question, therefore, of the recognition in the Gospels of an active Power or Principle of evil outside of man, and exercising influence over him. It may be said that our Lord nowhere makes known the existence of such an evil Power as a point of doctrine. He assumes the current belief among the Jews of His time, rather than sets forth any new doctrine on the subject. This is true. But it is equally true that He clearly assumes the reality of such a Power; and both in His intercourse with His disciples and in His arguments with His opponents, uses language the natural meaning of which places the reality of a kingdom of evil beyond dispute.

With any further questions pertaining to the character of this kingdom, the personality of its head and subordinate members, their origin, their agency, and mode of influence, we are not now concerned. These questions do not enter essentially into the consideration of our subject. It was necessary to bring so much into view, if for no other purpose than to show the somewhat different atmosphere as to the general question of evil which meets us in the New Testament. What at the utmost can only-be considered suggestions in the Old Testament, stand forth as clear intimations in the Christian Revelation. Evil is here before us from the first, and prominently, not merely as a characteristic of humanity and the moral atmosphere in which humanity moves, but as a supernatural element of affecting the world and man from the outside. Temptation is no longer merely a reality, addressing man's sense or soliciting man's will--that lies in its nature always--but it is a living Power, the representative of a kingdom hostile to the Divine, and hostile to man as the offspring of the Divine. All this may be equally true from the beginning, and may, as our dogmatic systems suppose, be the only adequate explanation of the primary sin and fall of man. But the fact is not made clear in the Old

The Christian Doctrine of Sin

Testament by itself--is not made to fix our attention as in the New. Here only it is we meet in full the idea of a Power of evil fronting the Divine in implacable hostility, and encompassing man as his everactive enemy and tempter.

It is important, at the same time, to notice how the idea of such a Power in the New Testament, however it may be designated or described, is discriminated from the evil Principle of the Persian religion to which we formerly adverted, and with which it has by certain writers been confounded, or at least brought into comparison. Some have not hesitated to trace the origin of the New Testament conception to the intercourse of the Jews with the Persians, and the influence naturally exercised upon them by Persian modes of thought. It is difficult to say whether the Jewish mind did not receive some impulse towards the whole subject of Angelology, and especially the existence of evil spirits, from their Persian neighbours, or the general stream of thought regarding the Supernatural which was filtrating from this quarter into the religious mind of the time. As with other curious questions lying alongside of our subject, we do not venture to enter upon this, and the less reluctantly that nothing definite or satisfactory can be said regarding it. This, however, is plainly evident, that the Jewish conception of Satan is greatly distinguished from the Zoroastrian conception of Ahriman (Anra-Mainyus). The latter is a twin spirit with Ormuzd (Ahura-Mazda), the good Power--apparently coequal, and no less concerned than the good in the production of the world. The warfare of the two is a warfare as of balanced forces. The world and human nature are conceived as arising out of their joint action or conflict. On the contrary, Satan is represented everywhere in the New Testament as indeed the enemy of God, yet subordinate and inferior to Him. His power is a real power; it is a power of dread and danger, capable of assailing Jesus himself, "the Holy One and the Just:" yet it is always limited and subordinate to a higher divine purpose. [86] Above all, it has no control of man, save through his own yielding. Evil, in short, even as impersonated in Satan, can only get near to man along the line of his own will. The Evil has no creative or original share in him. Satan is not, like Anra-Mainyus, concerned in his being from the first: and no part of his being, material or spiritual, is essentially evil, or a necessary prey to evil influence. The idea of matter as in itself evil, or the hopeless sphere of evil, underlies not only the Persian mythology, but all the numerous modes of thought so rife in the first ages of the Church, which have more or less affinity to it. There is not a trace of this in the Gospels. The Powers of evil, with Satan at their head, are everywhere conceived as moral Powers-Powers lying outside of the material cosmos, and while working through it, in no sense embedded within it or identified with it. The essential morality of the evangelical conception separates it, therefore, entirely from the Persian, and places it on a higher level.

This point is all the more significant, that the Persian conception of matter as hopelessly corrupt, and itself the evil, had beyond doubt extended itself in the time of our Lord, within the sphere of Judaism, and formed a characteristic tenet of one of its three prominent sects. The Essenes were not only ascetics, separated from both Pharisees and Sadducees by certain practical observances regarding food and marriage, and other social restrictions, but, as recent investigation has clearly shown, [87] were also Gnostics, animated in their ascetical rigidities by the speculative principle of the abhorrence of matter as the abode of evil. This idea, therefore, like many others, was in the intellectual atmosphere of the time; and if certain modern views of the origin of Christianity were true, it would almost certainly have been found in the Gospels. Yet, as we have said, there is not a trace of it there. The taint of Nature-religion is entirely absent, even where the thought of the Gospels comes directly into contact with the thought of the age, circulating from Aryan no less than Semitic, sources. It does not cling even to the skirts of the evangelical doctrine. The conception of Satan, like every other element of revealed religion, is a moral and not a natural conception, having all its true life and influence within the higher sphere.

And this also it is which renders it unnecessary that we should dwell further upon the background of evil brought out so prominently in the Gospels and throughout the New Testament Scriptures. Whatever conclusions we may form as to its character and influence, cannot affect the special truths which sum up the Christian doctrine of sin. Whatever be the Power or Powers of evil outside of man recognised in the New Testament, sin remains in its contents essentially the same. The hidden Powers of evil supposed to encompass man can only assail him from within. Their influence is spiritual, and is only operative within the free spiritual life which belongs to every man. This is the constant representation of the New Testament. There is no element of necessity or constraint in the picture of diabolic influence; or, if there is, by the very same fact, the idea of sin disappears, and that of mere misfortune or calamity emerges. In short, whatever be its accidents, sin is seen as clearly as ever--and, indeed, more clearly than ever--to be rooted in the personal will of man--the product of his own self-determining agency. It appears, if not more plainly, yet more fully, as the wilful transgression of law which is divine, not merely by imposition, but by intuition. God Himself is brought more close to the individual conscience as Authority and Lawgiver, but also, and especially, as Father,--a living Spirit of Love, whose will is at once man's law and man's good.

1. In the representation of sin given by our Lord in the Gospels, the first point that claims attention is the manner in which He intensifies the Old Testament idea of it, as deviation from or transgression of

law. The expressions used to describe sin are the direct equivalents in Greek of the Hebrew expressions noticed in last Lecture. The most general expression conveys the same idea of failure or missing a mark as the Hebrew expression chattath formerly discussed. [88] This is the expression used in the case of the "man sick of the palsy," whom our Lord cures in the opening of His ministry: "Son, be of good cheer; thy sins [89] be forgiven thee." Again, in the well-known passage, "Wherefore I say unto you, Every sin[90] and blasphemy shall be forgiven unto men; but the blasphemy against the Holy Ghost shall not be forgiven unto men." Again, very expressively, "Whosoever committeth sin is the servant of sin;" [91] and, "And when He is come, He will reprove the world of sin." [92] The expression rendered by our translators "iniquity," and which more precisely means negation or violation of law, is also used in St. Matthew, both with and without the article--as, for example, in the following passages: "Depart from me, ye that work iniquity;" "They" (the angels) "shall gather out of His kingdom all things that offend, and them which do iniquity." [93] The Pharisees are said to be "full of hypocrisy and iniquity." [94] The original of the familiar word trespasses, [95] so associated with the Lord's Prayer, deserves also to be mentioned in connection with the Gospels. The expression, however, does not occur in the Lord's Prayer itself; either in St. Matthew or St. Luke, but in the significant verses immediately following the prayer in St. Matthew's Gospel, [96] and the corresponding passage in St. Mark. [97] The expression used in the Lord's Prayer in the first Gospel is peculiar, and marks a peculiar shade of meaning--viz., "debts;" [98] the idea being that sins are chargeable against us as debts are, and that, if not forgiven, they must be paid in full. The language of the prayer as given in the Gospel of St. Luke, less frequently used than other forms of it, brings out the close connection betwixt sins designated by the ordinary expression and the idea of indebtedness: "And forgive us our sins, for we also forgive every one that is indebted to us."[99]

Such is the general description of sin in the Gospels, answering nearly to what we have already found in the Old Testament. But a mere enumeration of words and their specific meanings gives but a poor account of the deeper meaning which our Lord's teaching throws into the subject. It is only when we bring into view this higher conception of the standard or law which marks failure, deviation, or transgression, that we see how far more penetrating is His conception of sin, even as a breach of law.

The law was not to Him, as it had become to the ordinary Jewish mind of whatever school--a mere letter of commands or of prohibitions: "Honour thy father and thy mother;" "Thou shalt not kill;" "Thou shalt not commit adultery;" "Thou shalt not forswear thyself." He did not disparage its literal meaning; but its true meaning was far deeper than the letter. The law was for Him a spiritual ideal, "quick and powerful," like the word of God in the Epistle to the Hebrews, [100] "and sharper than any two-edged sword, piercing even to the dividing asunder of soul and spirit, and of the joints and marrow,"--"a discerner of the thoughts and intents of the heart." It is not enough that men keep within the letter, and in its sense do no violence or commit no impurity; but men are no less transgressors if they cherish angry feelings against a brother, or look on a woman to lust after her. The law, so far from being destroyed, is glorified and fulfilled in His teaching; and sin, or its violation, stands forth not merely as an outward act, but as an inward thought or inclination.: The principle of law being thus spiritualised, the principle of its negation is equally spiritualised. The conditions of righteousness and purity binding our being are no mere external conditions, restraining the outward activities, but conditions of the soul-- necessary and absolute forms of its life--within which its most secret movements, no less than its outward manifestations, must circulate. Whatever be the origin of our ideas of law and right--whether they come to us from without or within--our Lord does not meddle with such questions; they exist. They are summarily comprehended in the Ten Commandments. But not only so; the law is nigh to us--in our heart. It binds our inmost being no less than our external conduct. It extends absolutely over every sphere of our voluntary activity. The ancient words only mirror an ideal right that lives in every conscience not "dead in sin;" and sin begins not only when the letter of the law is broken, but when the ideal is obscured within and the heart has sunk deliberately below its own highest conception of right.

2. But not merely is the conception of law, and of sin as its violation, thus idealised and extended in our Lord's teaching; the conception of God as the giver of the law, and hence of sin as personal disobedience against its Author, is at the same time more clearly brought out. The Divine is not only an external authority commanding us, but a living Will that claims our service. We are to keep the commandments, not merely because it is right for us to do so, because the law is a categorical imperative within us which will not let us do as we will, but, above all, because it is God Himself that is ruling us by His law. His is the voice which speaks in the ancient words, and in the response which our hearts make to the words. He is Himself the immediate object of all moral obligation. We are to obey Him, not merely because His commands lie upon us, but because He is the Author and Father of our being, in whom alone we live and move--whose we are, and to whom we owe all. And our sin is consequently not merely "transgression of law," but disobedience against Him--rejection of His will.

This essential aspect of sin as involving offence against a living Will no less than deviation from a right rule, is abundantly present in the Old Testament, and especially in the prophetic writings and the Psalms. It was inseparably involved in the whole character of Hebraism as a theocracy--a system which clothed itself in the form of law, but of which God was everywhere the immediate centre. It was nothing new, therefore, to the Hebrew consciousness. This has been clearly seen already. A Jew could hardly ever, amidst all the traditions of Pharisaism, lose sight of the relation of his sin to God as well as to the law. But the experience is everywhere requickened in our Lord's teaching; and all who heard Him were made to feel that their conduct had not merely a legal but a personal bearing. There was One ever with them, seeing them not only as their fellow-men saw them, but seeing them in secret; [101] knowing what they had need of before they asked Him, [102] their "Father in heaven;"--and all that they thought and did was judged by Him with unerring judgment. All their evil, therefore, was sin against Him. It was a rejection of His will as well as an offence against His authority. It was not only disorder, but undutifulness.

3. And this leads us to a higher element of our Lord's teaching than we have yet reached. The law is not only idealised, and the conception of the divine personality everywhere made prominent, but there is a clearer, if not a wholly new, revelation made of the Divine. The Supreme Being is not merely moral order centred in a personal will, but moral perfection. The Right that rules our lives is at the same time the Love that guides them. God is our Father in heaven, all whose will towards us is good. This is one of the highest notes of spiritual advance in the Gospels--the clear identification of righteousness and goodness, of law and of love. These two ideas, so apt to be separated--so frequently, in point of fact, separated in popular religion--are everywhere identical in Christ, and in the higher spiritual sphere revealed by Him. The God of whom He speaks is not only supreme, but supremely good. "He maketh His sun to rise on the evil and the good, and sendeth rain on the just and the unjust." [103] "If ye then, being evil, know how to give good gifts unto your children, how much more shall your Father which is in heaven give good things to them that ask Him!" [104] The idea of goodness is specially the idea of God. And yet divine goodness is never represented as good-nature, or mere complacency. On the contrary, it is inseparably bound up with righteousness and truth. A love without justice would prove to be no love at all. A goodness without holiness would be a mere shadow, on which no true heart could rest. Love is the innermost principle of the Divine, but the Divine is always the Right. Goodness without morality is unintelligible in the spiritual sphere. Within this sphere they are not only inseparable, they are essentially coherent--twin aspects of the same spiritual perfection. Right is Love, however it may sometimes seem disguised in the face of wrong; and Love, on the other hand, embraces every essential principle of morality. Hence the Divine is all summed up in Love. It is the secret of moral order in heaven and on earth. It is the name for the highest, alike in God and in man--the complete expression for the law above us, and the complete expression for the law within us. "God is love." [105] "Love is the fulfilling of the law." [106] When the Pharisees were gathered together, one of them, a lawyer, "asked Him a question, tempting Him, and saying, Master, which is the great commandment in the law? Jesus said unto him, Thou shalt love the Lord thy God with all thy heart, and with all thy soul, and with all thy mind. This is the first and great commandment. And the second is like unto it, Thou shalt love thy neighbour as thyself. On these two commandments hang all the law and the prophets." [107] As love in God is the sum of moral perfection, love in us towards God and towards our neighbour is the sum of all moral duty.

This higher teaching of Christ reflects everywhere a deeper shadow on human sin. If divine righteousness be always divine goodness, and the law, even in its most restrictive aspects, be only a form of concealed love working for our good, the wilful violation of law and of right is at the same time enmity against the Good. This thought is frequently repeated in the Gospels. In the profound and beautiful parable of the prodigal son--which is throughout full of meaning for our subject--it is specially apparent. It is the deepest offence of the prodigal, not that he had yielded to the lawless impulses of self-indulgence--wasted his substance in riotous living, and broken the laws of temperance and purity--nor even that he has sinned against a parental authority which claimed his obedience; but that, as his own heart at length tells him, he has done despite to a father's love, and offended against a goodness which was following him solicitously amid all his wilful degradation, and waiting all along to welcome his return. [108] Again, in the solemn passage [109] about blasphemy against the Holy Ghost, where our Lord is contending with pathetic indignation against the darkness of Pharisaic unbelief, it is this thought that marks the depth of His pathos, and gives meaning to His awful warning: the Pharisees were offenders not merely against Himself but against the full lustre of goodness--the light of the Divine--the presence of the Holy Ghost seen in His works. There might have been excuses for their not apprehending or acknowledging Him as the Messiah on His own appeal; but His works spoke for themselves as works of divine healing and beneficence. The spirit of Goodness--of God--breathed in them, and yet they said they were the works of Beelzebub, the prince of devils. The light that was in them being darkness, how great was their darkness! The deepest element of their sin was this hatred of the good. This was their blasphemy against the Holy Ghost. All other sin may be forgiven; but a disposition which calls evil good, and good evil--darkness light, and light darkness--is unforgivable in its nature. It is hopeless--beyond the operation of divine grace. And so the darkness of sin deepens as the light of God falls upon it. The shadows are cast more gloomily into the abysses of human self-will and alienation from the Divine, as the ideal of Love rises more luminously in the spiritual heavens.

John Tulloch, D.D.

The same aspect of our Lord's teaching serves to bring out more plainly the essential nature of sin. As love, or the going forth of the human will in harmony towards the Divine, is the highest expression of moral duty, so the opposite of all this, or the concentration of the will upon itself in opposition to the Divine, is the uttermost expression of sin. More than anything else, the essence of sin is to be found in concentrated self-will or perverted egoism. In such a case the will is not merely astray, or out of the right way. So far as any will may have thus deviated, there is always something of the nature of sin, but there also may be much of the nature of accident or misfortune. All wrong-doing is deviation, but all deviation may not proceed from a wrongful purpose. The mark may be missed, and the stumble made in the darkness of unconsciousness, under blind impulses for the moment irresistible. These cannot make wrong right, but they may infinitely excuse the wrong. The element of sin may barely exist in certain acts of deviation, so little relation may they have to the conscious personality of the agent. But where the will deliberately asserts itself in wrong,--choosing self-indulgence rather than self-control--self-interest even to a brother's hurt,--then sin appears in its true character. It marks itself as the opposite of what is known as love--the latter representing the harmony of our personal life with the Divine, the former the concentration of this life upon itself in some form or another. As love is self-forgetfulness in God, sin is self-assertion against Him. Always there is this insurrectionary movement of self more or less present, whatever particular form the sin may take. It is not the form that is essential, but the inner movement of self expressed in it. Let the outside be stripped away, this core remains; and this it is, or the self-will in an attitude of hostile erection to the Divine, which is essentially sin. Hence, too, the positive or affirmative character which is so radical a note of sin. The true unity of the Divine and the human, of which love is the symbol, is dissolved; but a false unity takes its place. The Divine ceases to be the centre; self becomes its own centre. [See [13]Appendix XIV.]

There is this inward penetration everywhere in our Lord's teaching, in the manner in which He deals with different classes of sinners, and the words with which He fixes attention, not on the outside but the inside of life. The Magdalene, and the Prodigal, and the Publican, are all sinners in His sight. They. have gone astray, and turned every one to his own way. Instead of the right they have chosen the wrong, and followed after vanity. Their sin, as all sin, is hateful to Him. He utters no word of leniency over it; yet he never speaks of it as he speaks of the sin of Pharisaic pride and Sadducean unbelief. The depth of impurity and profligacy does not move Him, like the depth of hypocrisy and hatred of the Good. There is alienation from the Divine in both cases; but the alienation is far more deliberate and self-concentrated in the one case than in the other. And while in the one He can say, "Go, and sin no more;" in the other He says, "Ye do the deeds of your father. . . . Ye are of your father the devil, and the lusts of your father ye will do." [110] He saw clearly to the heart, and discriminates the sin according to the degree of its evil in the self-will striving against the Divine. Similarly He speaks of all defilement as being from within, and not from without--a part of the self-life, and not of the accidental or external life. The external character should be without blame; but it is within the heart that the real character is formed. "Not that which goeth into the mouth defileth a man, but that which cometh out of the mouth, that defileth a man. . . . Those things which proceed out of the mouth come forth from the heart, and they defile the man. For out of the heart proceed evil thoughts, murders, adulteries, fornications, thefts, false-witness, blasphemies." [111] All these are but various forms of self-will turned away from the Divine, and falsely seeking to make a centre for itself. "These are the things which defile a man; but to eat with unwashen hands defileth not a man." [112]

4. There is a special aspect of sin, afterwards elaborated by St. Paul, which also appears in our Lord's teaching. He characterises it not merely in act and in essence, but as a condition and tendency of humanity. Man not only sins, but he is a sinner naturally. It is his nature and disposition to sin. "Every good tree bringeth forth good fruit; but a corrupt tree bringeth forth evil fruit." [113] "The tree is known by its fruit. O generation of vipers, how can ye, being evil, speak good things? for out of the abundance of the heart the mouth speaketh." [114] The import of such language, as well as other forms of language[115] -- even when bearing a special application--is sufficiently obvious. Sin is set forth as a disease or corruption of human nature. It is not merely an act, but a state which clings to the race, a tendency lying in our nature, and which is constantly coming forth into action. It is in the flesh--the product of the natural birth; and "that which is born of the flesh is flesh." [116] This doctrine of the "flesh" as the seat of sin will afterwards come before us fully in the writings of St. Paul. In the meantime, it is interesting to trace the definite allusion to it in the fourth Gospel. The idea is clearly announced, but it is only touched. In St. Paul we shall find it fully expanded.

5. Along with this, another aspect of sin is very prominent in the Gospels in connection with our Lord's miracles. Sin is not merely a disease or corruption of human nature, but it is closely associated with frightful forms of physical malady and human unhappiness. It leaves a deep stain of guilt and wretchedness which repeats itself in individuals, families, and nations. The sick of the palsy needs spiritual no less than physical healing. Nay, the key of the bodily cure is through the spiritual. "Whether is easier to say, Thy sins be forgiven thee; or to say, Arise, and walk?" [117] The demon-possessed are diseased in body as in mind-blind and dumb as well as insane and violent. [118] There is clearly implied in

The Christian Doctrine of Sin

our Lord's language [119] a mysterious affinity betwixt natural and moral evil. The latter bears with it not only its proper doom of alienation from all that is spiritually good, but carries with it, moreover, a frequent train of natural doom and disaster. It issues in many forms of guilt and misery, and casts its gloomy shadow far beyond its immediate subject. This aspect of sin will also again and more elaborately meet us in St. Paul; but it deserves to be noted here, not only because it is so far clearly indicated in our Lord's teaching, but because He has Himself also cautioned us against the arbitrary misuse of the principle which it involves. While the consequences of sin are so fatal in individuals and in families, passing over in many forms of inherited wretchedness from generation to generation, and showing its existence in physical no less than in moral calamity, we are not yet warranted in connecting natural and moral evil together in particular cases. "Or those eighteen, upon whom the tower of Siloam fell, and slew them, think ye that they were sinners above all men that dwelt in Jerusalem? I tell you, Nay; but, except ye repent, ye shall all likewise perish." [120] Again, in a well-known passage in the fourth Gospel: "Master, who did sin, this man, or his parents, that he was born blind? Jesus answered, Neither hath this man sinned, nor his parents: but that the works of God should be made manifest in him." [121] In other words--for this is what our Lord's teaching comes to in this matter--the punitive justice of God is a great fact. It is stamped on all the darker phenomena of human life-disease, insanity, and death. It is in the nature of sin to entail suffering, and work itself, as an element of punishment, into all the complicated web of human existence. But it is not ours to fix or apportion its blame. It is present in every form of suffering; but the incidence of suffering is no measure of individual demerit in the tangled spectacle of human existence.

6. Sin, which thus belongs to our nature, and cleaves to it so terribly, is necessarily universal. The language of the Psalmist, "There is no man that doeth good and sinneth not," is plainly the affirmation, if not in so many words, of Christ. He addresses His invitation of grace to all. He is come to seek and to save that which is lost. [122] The clear inference is, that all have sunk from the good which they ought to have--"All have sinned, and come short of the glory of God." [123] No doubt, there are passages also in which Christ seems to discriminate betwixt members of the human race as "evil and good," "just and unjust," [124] and where He would even seem to imply that there are those who have no need of His spiritual teaching,--"They that are whole need not a physician, but they that are sick. I came not to call the righteous, but sinners to repentance." [125] But such passages are plainly capable of an explanation, which leaves the fact of universal sinfulness without challenge. They find their explanation in the fact, that our Lord's language, here and everywhere, is not the language of theological analysis, but of common life. And as we say that there are good and bad men in the world, without meaning to affirm that there are any men without sin, so the Gospels speak of the evil and the good, the just and the unjust. The "honest and good heart" which receives the truth is not a heart in which there is no evil, but one in which the evil has not so hardened and shut out the work of the Spirit as to prevent its responding to the force of the truth when presented to it. There may still be another meaning in such words of the Lord, as that He came not to call the righteous, but sinners to repentance--a meaning not without a latent touch of satire, if we can imagine such a thing. The "righteous" in His time was something of a phrase. There were those like the Pharisees who made a profession of righteousness, "going about to establish their own righteousness." [126] Our Lord might say that He came not to call these--not that they did not need His call, but because they thought themselves too good to need it. They were after their own views, perfect in legal righteousness, and they knew of no other. There was nothing in them, any more than there was in those altogether hardened in evil, to respond to His call. In the one class the spiritual consciousness was dead, in the other it was self-satisfied. The call of a Saviour could reach neither till the depths of personal feeling were stirred in them, and the distress of sin arose from these depths as something too hard to be borne.

This spiritual susceptibility is everywhere presupposed as a condition of receiving divine grace and truth. But the absence of the susceptibility is not to be held as an evidence that we do not need both--in other words, that we are not sinners. The fact that we have no sense of our need--that we have never cried "out of the depths," "If thou, Lord, shouldst mark iniquities, O Lord, who shall stand?"--this, to say the least, only proves, not that we have no sin, but that we have failed to realise the responsibilities of our spiritual life--that we have been living upon the surface of intellectual and social conventions, and have never got down to the depth of our own spiritual being, or fronted the dreadful realities of sin, righteousness, and judgment. It was easy to the Pharisee and Scribe in the time of our Lord--it may be easy to the intellectualist and the man of the world now--to dwell within the levels of their own conventional thought, and feel from these levels as if a call to repentance had for them no meaning. But let the levels once be broken up, the fountains of their deeper life unsealed, and the waters thereof roar and be troubled, and then the spiritual call will be found to have an answer in their hearts, and facts more real than any their conventions have ever measured will find an utterance within them. Let it be remembered, although it is often forgotten, that Christianity always takes human nature at the fullest--in its complete mass of need, feeling, and aspiration. It is not man as Pharisee or Sadducee, as intellectualist or mystic or sensualist, but man as containing in himself the potencies of all these--as a

John Tulloch, D.D.

being of manifold complex energy, with work and ambitions on earth, but with aspirations towards heaven. Within such a full-souled being, awake to his true position in the world, there will always be--the Gospel assumes--the sense of sin, the self-witness of having erred, and strayed, and done evil before the eye of Divine Purity, that searches us through and through, although it looks not on our sin.

7. But this view of the subject suggests a further and final characteristic of our Lord's teaching regarding sin, which it is important to notice. While man is everywhere a sinner before Him who was Himself "holy, harmless, undefiled," yet he is nowhere represented as nothing but a sinner. "There is no man that doeth good and sinneth not" in the Gospels any more than elsewhere in Scripture. But the Gospels are singularly free from those exaggerated colours in which a later theology has sometimes drawn human nature. Man is a fallen and degraded being. He is at the best, be he Pharisee or Publican, among the "lost" whom Christ came to seek and to save. But he is noble even in his degradation. There is a capacity of divine life in him, beneath all the ruin of his nature. He is godlike, even with the image of his divine original broken and defaced. The divine likeness is obscured, but not obliterated. It may be traced amidst all the accumulations of sinful ruin. The very misery of man, as Pascal has said--interpreting this aspect of our Lord's teaching--attests his true greatness. He is a king dethroned, but still a king. The crown has fallen from his head, its gold has become dim and its most fine gold changed, but there is the faint lustre of it yet on his brow, and the dignity of having once worn it still lives in his heart. There is nothing more characteristic of our Lord's teaching than this recognition of the divine original of humanity, and of the divine potency which still survives in it. This is the only key to His redemptive mission. He came to recover the fallen, and to set up that which had been thrown down. He saw what was in man more truly than all others. He saw the possibilities of restoration in the demoniac and the Magdalene--the promise of an eternal life in the trustfulness of the thief upon the cross--the divine sparks still living amidst all the waste of ruined lives. The cry of the returning prodigal was heard by Him a far way off; and even while he ate of the husks and grovelled with the swine, the thought of his divine home had not died out of him, and the capacity of return had not absolutely perished.

Dark as sin ever is, therefore, in the view of our Lord, and fallen as human nature is, it is not yet, as it has been sometimes represented, a mere mass of corruption. The tone which could say of it that it contains nothing but sin, and produces nothing which is not damnable, [See [14]Appendix XV.] is foreign to the Gospels. Such language, even in its extravagance, may represent a true side of human nature--human nature in entire divorce from the Divine--but certainly not a fair picture of human life. The higher vision of Christ embraces not only one side but all sides of humanity, and penetrates beneath all surface manifestations to its inner secrets. And therefore His view is always at once compassionate and comprehensive--stern, yet gracious. He sees man not merely as he is or seems to be, but as he is capable of being. His vision is complete and creative. It takes in the end from the beginning; and from amidst the broken and ruined fragments of the divine original beholds arising again, under His redeeming touch and the quickening power of His regenerating Spirit, new shapes of spiritual excellence--the new man, created after His own image in knowledge, righteousness, and holiness.

As one has said, speaking of this subject, in words so fitly and eloquently descriptive that we may close this Lecture with them:--

"Not half a century ago a great man was seen stooping and working in a charnel-house of bones. Uncouth, nameless fragments lay around him, which the workmen had dug up and thrown aside as rubbish. They belonged to some far back ages; and no man knew what they were or whence. Few men cared. The world was merry at the sight of a philosopher groping among mouldy bones. But when that creative mind, reverently discerning the fontal types of being in diverse shapes, brought together those strange fragments, bone to bone, and rib to claw, and both to its corresponding vertebrae, recombining the wondrous forms of past ages, and presenting each to the astonished world as it lived and moved a hundred thousand years back, then men began to perceive that a new science had begun on earth. And such was the creative [vision and] work of Christ. He took the scattered fragments of our ruined nature, interpreted their meaning, showed the original intent of those powers which were now only destructive--drew out from publicans and sinners yearnings which were incomprehensible, feelings which were misunderstood--vindicated the beauty of their original intention, showed the divine order below the chaos, and exhibited to the world once more a human soul in the form in which God had made it, saying to the dry bones, live." [127]

Footnotes:
75. Rev. xx. 2.
76. "And Satan stood up against Israel, and provoked David to number Israel." The expression is here used without the article, and may be translated, as elsewhere, simply as "adversary."
77. Job, i. 6, 12; ii. 1.
78. Matt. xvi. 23, where our Lord addresses St. Peter, "Get thee behind me, Satan," or adversary.
79. Matt. iv. 1, 5, 8, 11; xiii. 39: "Tempter," Matt. iv. 3; Luke iv. 2, 3, 5, 6, 13; John viii. 44.
80. Matt. iv. 10; xii. 26; Mark i. 13; iii. 23, 26; iv. I5; Luke, iv. 8.

81. Matt. xii. 24; Mark iii. 22.
82. Matt. xii. 24.
83. Matt. xii. 29.
84. Matt. xiii. 38.
85. Matt. xiii. 39.
86. Matt. iv. 1; Rev. xii. 12, xv. 2.
87. See quotation in [15]Appendix XIII. from Dr. Lightfoot's interesting chapter on this subject in his recent Commentary on the Colossians.
88. Hamartia, failure (its original etymology is uncertain), stands for sin in general in the New Testament, as cht't in the Old Testament; and, associated with this general expression, there is a "mournfully numerous group" of words analogous to the Old Testament group formerly considered, and expressing more or less the same definite shades of meaning. It is unnecessary to add any critical discussion of these words beyond that given in the text. The three there mentioned--viz., hamartia, hanomia, paraptoma--are all used by our Lord,--the first, however, by far the most frequently. (Hamartema is found in Mark, iii. 28, and doubtfully in Mark, iv. 12.) Anomia is used with great significance in the First Epistle of St. John, iii. 4, in conjunction with hamartia: Pas ho poion ten hamartian kai ten anomian poiei; kai he hamartia estin he anomia--Whosoever committeth sin transgresseth also the law: for sin is the transgression of the law." Paraptoma is often employed by St. Paul; Rom. v. 15, 16, 17, 18, 20; Eph. ii. 1; Gal. vi. 1. Expressions specially Pauline are parakoe ("disobedience to a voice "), opposed to hupakoe (Rom. v. 19; 2 Cor. x. 6; Heb. ii. 2); parabasis ("transgression ") very frequently (Rom. ii. 23, v. 14; 1 Tim. ii. 14; Heb. ii. 2--in conjunction with parakoe, Heb. ix. 15). Readers anxious to study the several shades of meaning which have been associated with these words may be referred to Archbishop Trench's volume on New Testament Synonyms, second part, p. 61, 73. It is evident, from the interesting discussion and quotation of authorities there given, that too much is not to be made of these shades of meaning, and that the full force of the evangelical and Pauline thought on the subject is better gathered by a comprehensive induction of the leading particulars of this thought, such as is attempted in the Lectures, than by any mere critical analysis of words.
89. Hamartiai--Matt. ix. 2, 5.
90. Pasa hamartia, "all manner of sin"--Matt. xii. 31.
91. Ten hamartian . . . tes hamartias--John, viii. 34.
92. Peri hamartias--John, xvi. 8.
93. Matt. vii. 23, xiii. 41.
94. Matt. xxiii. 28, anomia. In the first two passages quoted in the text, the expression occurs with the article, ten anomian--in the third, it occurs without the article.
95. Paraptoma.
96. Matt. vi. 14, 15.
97. Mark, xi. 25, 26.
98. Opheilemata.
99. Luke, xi. 4, hamartias . . . panti opheilonti hemin;
100. Heb. iv. 12.
101. Matt vi. 4, 6.
102. Matt. vi. 8.
103. Matt. v. 45.
104. Matt. vii. 11.
105. 1 John, iv. 8.
106. Rom. xiii. 10.
107. Matt. xii. 35-40.
108. Luke, xv. 11-32.
109. Matt. xii. 31, 32.
110. John viii. 11, 41, 44.
111. Matt. xv. 1, 18. 19.
112. Matt. xv. 20.
113. Matt. vii. 17.
114. Matt. xii. 33, 34.
115. Matt. ix. 12.
116. John, iii. 6.
117. Matt. ix. 5.
118. Matt. viii. 28, xii. 22; Mark, v. 2-13.
119. See also Luke, v. 20; John v. 14.
120. Luke, xiii. 4, 5.
121. John, ix. 2, 3.

122. Luke, xix. 10.
123. Rom. iii. 23.
124. Matt. v. 45.
125. Luke v. 31, 32.
126. Rom. x. 3.
127. Sermons by the late Rev. F. W. Robertson. Second Series. "On Christ's Estimate of Sin," p. 199, 200.

V - DOCTRINE OF ST. PAUL'S EPISTLES

IT requires but little insight to recognise the difference of our Lord's form of teaching in the Gospels, and that of St. Paul in his Epistles. In the former case we have for the most part concrete statements or pictures. The moral truth of Judaism and the higher truths of the Gospel are described in life and character. They come before us in authoritative announcement or living form, in graphic incident or pictured parable. Sin and righteousness are alike embodied in vivid representation. Even in the Sermon on the Mount, and elsewhere where our Lord appears directly as an instructor, and where, as we have seen, He develops the idea of sin, amplifying and deepening it, in contrast to His own spiritual ideal, as a spiritual state or attitude, and not merely an external act or breach of the letter of the law, He does so not by explanation or argument, but by revealed assertion and authority. He sets forth the fact--His higher conception of the divine law on the one hand, and His deeper and more spiritual conception of sin on the other hand. He does not deal in analysis or definition.

Nowhere in Scripture are the lines of the Good and of the Evil drawn more firmly or brought into sharper and clearer antagonism than in the Gospels. We feel as we read them everywhere the vivid breath of moral life and death. Sin in all its phases comes out in striking reality in His presence who is the "Light of the world." The forces of evil, whether embodied in Pharisee or Sadducee, in Herodian or Scribe, in Magdalene or Prodigal, in high priest or Roman governor, are distinctly and powerfully conceived, so that we can have no doubt of their features,--what it is to be good and what it is to be evil--what it is to be at one with the Divine, and what it is to be opposed to it. But withal, the teaching is by affirmation or example rather than by definition--by synthesis rather than by analysis. This is our Lord's manner: "Verily, verily, I say unto you." He taught as one "having authority, and not as the Scribes." His lessons were like the lessons of nature--graphic, living, comprehensive--addressed to the eye as well as the thought--majestic in their simplicity, inexhaustible in their divine fulness of meaning.

It is very different with St. Paul. He is a great preacher, but he is still more characteristically a great Christian scribe or writer. The fulness of divine truth is broken up in him into its several parts. It does not dwell in him bodily. It is not set forth by him-as in the Gospels--in creative and ideal types. St. Paul had been trained in the Jewish schools. He had been a "Hebrew of the Hebrews--as touching the law a Pharisee." He was familiar not merely with the living aspects of Jewish thought and character, but with the argumentative subtleties of the one, and the practical casuistries of the other. He was accustomed to find definitions for his opinions, and arguments for his assertions. He was a scholastic in intellect, if a missionary in enthusiasm. His manner, in calm statement, is essentially dialectical. And so we find, as we might expect to find, the more simple and concrete teaching of the Gospels not only expanded in the Pauline Epistles, but defined and analysed, and, if we may say so, rationalised and set forth in its several elements in their intellectual and spiritual relation to one another.

Our business is only with St. Paul's doctrine of sin; but his doctrine on this subject is closely intertwined with his system of doctrine, and especially with his central doctrine of righteousness by faith, and his vivid, if varying, conception of the law. It is necessary, so far, to bring into view his general system of thought, in order to understand the full meaning of his doctrine of sin.

The two great ideas of righteousness and law were typical ideas of the Hebrew mind. They were essentially correlated, and the one can only be understood in connection with the other. So soon as we touch the sphere of Revelation we come prominently within the range of moral law; we find ourselves in face of a divine Will, and of human wills rightfully subject to it. This is an infinitely higher stage of thought than any attained within the sphere of natural religion, or of religion outside of Revelation. But whether admitted to be higher or not, there can be no doubt of the fact that the Old Testament is everywhere the Revelation of a divine Will dealing with human wills; and the tenor of this Revelation is that the human will can only find its happiness in harmony with the Divine. This harmony of the Divine and human is righteousness: and the key-note of the Old Testament through all its pages is, that righteousness alone is blessedness. "Blessed is the man that walketh not in the counsel of the ungodly, nor standeth in the way of sinners. . . . But his delight is in the law of the Lord. . . . The Lord knoweth the way of the righteous; but the way of the ungodly shall perish." [128] "The word righteousness," as a modern writer [129] has said, "is the master-word of the Old Testament." "Blessed are they that keep judgment, and he that doeth righteousness." [130] "Cease to do evil; learn to do well." [131] "Stand in awe, and sin not. . . . Offer the sacrifices of righteousness, and put your trust in the Lord." [132] Here righteousness consists in obedience to law, or conformity of the human will to the Divine. To be right, is to be at one with God; to be wrong, is to be at variance with God. God is not only the head of the Hebrew theocracy--the divine source from which it came--but He is a living presence through all its manifestations and activities. The divine Will was supposed to be immediately expressed in every channel of the Hebrew law and prophets--as much in one channel, or part of it, as another. "The law, the fulfilment of the law" (righteousness), "and the divine Author of the law, pass into each other. The mind is carried on imperceptibly from the one to the other." [133]

To us the divine law is specially the moral law, or the ten words or commandments of Moses. We distinguish betwixt what we call the ceremonial or the political law of the Jews, and the moral law. But the Jews themselves made no such distinction. The law was to them in their later history the whole law of Moses as contained in the Pentateuch. Nay, the term law assumed a still wider significance, and seems to have been identified with the whole letter of the Old Testament, as interpreted and applied by the Sopherim or Scribes. St. Paul uses the word in more senses than one. It has, we shall see, a higher or universal meaning for him, as well as a common meaning. But the common meaning which it bears for him, as for other Jews, is the whole Jewish or Old Testament system. [134] This was the law which he had known before his conversion, as touching which he was a Pharisee. And this is the law which plays such a part in his writings, in contrast to the Gospel and the freedom which the Gospel brings with it.

The mind of the Jew was impregnated by this idea of law. It was the law which made his religion. The two terms, or the two ideas, had become co-ordinate with him. He rested in the law, and made his boast of God as its Author. [135] It was to him a vast system, all equally of divine authorship. It is easy for us to trace and estimate the relation of its several parts, and to distinguish what is spiritual and permanent in it, from what is ceremonial and temporary. But this was the last thing of which a Jewish mind was capable. All in his religion seemed to the Jew equally sacred. It is the tendency of all national religion to take up into it much that is accidental and temporary, and to extend the same sanction of divine authority to all parts of its creed and ritual--the non-essential no less than the essential. And this tendency was one specially favored by the character of Judaism after the Captivity, and the prominence which it gave to the scholastic element in its exposition and diffusion. St. Paul inherited this tendency in its full force as a typical Jew--"a Hebrew of the Hebrews." The Jewish law had been to him, at least, all that it was to other Jews of his time. He seems jealous that any should be able to say that they prized it more than he had done; that they understood it better, or placed a more extended and significant meaning upon it. If it had been possible to be saved by the law--by appreciation of its divine character, by faithful and zealous obedience to its prescriptions--he would have found that salvation. As touching the righteousness which is in the law, he held himself blameless.

When St. Paul speaks specially of the law, therefore, in contrast to the Gospel, he means the whole Jewish law. He did not, as we are now in the habit of doing, discriminate its parts, or separate them in their historical development and relative importance, any more than the other Jews of his time. What he did, and what distinguished him as a spiritual thinker and teacher, was something far more important than this. He saw that the idea of law was not limited by its Jewish conception. The thought in which he had been bred clung to him. Judaism was to him a great system of antique growth, and venerable in all its parts. He had faithfully tried to find religious life within the system, and yielded to none in the admiration with which he had regarded it.: But all the while he had been learning that the thought of God was greater than any system. And when he became a Christian he saw this clearly. He saw that God had never left Himself without a witness on the earth; and that what He had been specially doing for the Jewish people by the law, He had been more or less doing for all people by the voice of reason and the monitions of conscience.

While the law, therefore, remained to St. Paul what he had been trained to esteem it--the whole sphere of the theocratic institutions (only seen in a more spiritual light)--yet it lost for him its exclusiveness. It took its place, not as the whole of the divine plan for man's spiritual education, which, before his conversion, it had seemed to him as well as to other Jews, but only as a phase of that plan, preceded by the divine promise to Abraham, and supplemented by all the indications of natural reason and conscience outside of Judaism. The idea of law, in short, was for him expanded and broadened in a sense unknown to Pharisaism. It became a universal principle of moral order encompassing all life, however dimly known or realised. The Jews had enjoyed a special Revelation. The Divine had been made clear to them in definite command and precept,--"Line upon line, precept upon precept." This was their privilege and boast. There could be no doubt, therefore, of their responsible relation to the Divine. The only doubt was whether the Divine had not been obscured to them by the very multiplicity of the sanctions which had been drawn from it--whether they had not lost the quick sense of the spiritual in the manifoldness of the letter. But the fact of a divine Ideal was something which all nations might have known--an undeniable reality revealed in nature, and cognisable by reason and conscience. The invisible things of God were to be clearly seen in creation and providence by all discerning and devout hearts. Reverence for the Divine, and obedience to it, were therefore obligatory within the pale of Gentilism no less than of Judaism. The absence of a special Revelation, or definite form of divine law, did not leave men excused in their violations of duty. There was the capacity in all men of reaching to a knowledge of the Divine, and of a higher divine order; and this, in the absence of definite divine institutions, was a law in itself. "For when the Gentiles, which have not the law, do by nature the things contained in the law these having not the law are a law unto themselves." [136] Here the common and higher meaning of the word appear together; and the apostle passes rapidly from the one to the other, the great thought in both cases being that there is a moral order behind all moral life, and that the truth and rightness of the life are only found in consistency with the order.

This is the backbone, so to speak, of all St. Paul's thought, as indeed of that Hebrew thought which he so prominently represented. He was not less but more a Hebrew in that he was capable of rising above the Jewish stand-point of his time, and embracing not only the chosen race but the human race within his moral Ideal. The Jews were especially the children of law. They had been placed under special divine tutelage and government, for the very purpose that the idea of divine authority might be brought home to the human mind, and made a living part of it. Their system of policy and government, therefore, was especially the law, and it was difficult for the ordinary Jewish mind to conceive of divine authority apart from a system which was for it equivalent to the Divine. St. Paul did not himself see beyond it for a time. But when the broader vision came to him, it was not by losing the moral depth of his early faith, but by understanding and realising it more clearly. He did not, in other words, pass out of Hebraism to a less serious view of humanity; but he extended its essential thought so as to embrace humanity. The principle of divine authority which his national religion had nurtured was set free in his mind from the restraints in which he and other Jewish teachers had been accustomed to regard it, and was felt to be a universal principle lying at the root of all human happiness and all moral progress.

It is in the light of this principle of law or moral order that St. Paul views all mankind, and that his doctrine of sin is set forth in its several aspects. Carrying with him this principle, he applied it to Jew and Gentile alike, and pronounced all men to be sinners. With reference to the same principle, more or less, he unfolded the nature and the effects of sin. The main points of the Pauline doctrine will arrange themselves naturally under three successive heads: 1st, The universality of sin; 2d, The nature or seat of sin; and, 3d, The effects or consequences of sin. St. Paul has a great deal to say on all these points that it concerns us to know, and his manner of teaching them is all the more interesting that it involves throughout an appeal to experience. Granting to him the principle which lies behind all his thought, and which it was the great function of Hebraism to plant in the human consciousness, that man is a moral being subject to divine authority--in other words, a subject of law--St. Paul works out his doctrine of sin in the main experimentally. He takes man, and, placing him in the mirror of divine law, shows him all the ruin and sadness of his moral state. He appeals against himself to facts of experience which admit of no denial; and lays bare the hidden folds of his moral consciousness with a keenness of psychological analysis that penetrates to the roots of his spiritual nature. We receive his words as words of divine authority; but they derive a peculiar interest and power from the manner in which they bring us into contact with spiritual facts, and clothe themselves with a life of experience which all higher minds may verify. It is in the great Epistle to the Romans that St. Paul especially unfolds his doctrine of sin, and to which our attention, therefore, will be mainly confined in this and the following Lecture.

1. In the opening of the epistle, St. Paul brings mankind, both Jew and Gentile, to the bar of moral judgment. He sets them in the light of that divine righteousness which had been growing in the' consciousness of the devout Israelite for centuries, and which had received such a powerful illustration in the life and death of Christ. This righteousness was a subject of Revelation. Man had not reached it by his own tentative moral gropings or ideas. It had come forth from God, the expression of His character and will, and had only been attainable always through a living relation to Him--in other words, through faith. The life of the righteous spoken of in the Old Testament was, in its highest form, not a life of moral effort, but of divine receptivity, as when Habakkuk says that "the just shall live by his faith." [137] But the actual state, both of the Gentile and the Jewish world, was infinitely removed from this life of righteousness, which is only realized through faith in the Divine. And with the view of showing this, he turns first to the moral state of the Gentiles. He speaks of what he sees around him. There is no reason to suppose that he exaggerates the picture of ungodliness and immorality which he draws with so powerful a pencil.

As the life of righteousness or moral order was the realisation of the divine Will for man, so the life of unrighteousness and moral disorder was the reverse of this, and therefore hateful to God. As the one was the object of divine complacency, the other was the object of divine wrath. And as St. Paul looked abroad over the Gentile world, he saw everywhere the revelation of this wrath against the abounding enormities of human sin. [138] Nor could the Gentiles plead ignorance of the Divine in excuse of their impiety and unrighteousness. On the contrary, the very strength of his accusation against them is that they hindered, obscured, and obstructed the truth by their unrighteousness. [139] The Divine was sufficiently made known to them. God had Himself made it known in the works of nature and in the instincts of the Divine originally planted within their hearts. The apostle clearly indicates the fact of man being able to reach the knowledge of the Divine without a special or positive Revelation. There is a

John Tulloch, D.D.

faculty of God-knowledge in man originally, a susceptibility of higher truth, for the use of which man is responsible, and for the abuse of which he is condemnable. "That which may be known of God is manifest in them; for God hath showed it unto them. For the invisible things of Him from the creation of the world are clearly seen, being understood by the things that are made, even His eternal power and Godhead; so that they are without excuse." [140] There is that in man, call it reason or conscience, which, looking out upon the world, ought to see in it the expression of divine thought and energy-of a living and eternal Mind; and the primary root of sin in the Gentiles was that they had allowed the revelation of the Divine to be utterly obscured in them. Made capable of knowing God, and having around them a constant witness of His eternal power and Godhead, they failed to glorify Him as God, or to cherish feelings of reverence or thankfulness towards the divine Author of their being and of the world. "They became vain in their imaginations, and their foolish heart was darkened. Professing themselves to be wise, they became fools, and changed the glory of the incorruptible God into an image made like to corruptible man, and to birds, and four-footed beasts, and creeping things. Wherefore God also gave them up to uncleanness through the lusts of their own hearts." [141]

The source of sin in the Gentile world was this obscuration of the idea of God. Man having sunk away from God, necessarily sank away from the life of righteousness which was only to be found in the knowledge of the divine character, and conformity to the divine will. The truth which they might have known they hindered, and changed into a lie. [142] Abjuring the creative Will, and turning away from its manifestations, they fell under the dominion of the creature. Nature took the place of the Divine in their hearts; and the consequences are pictured with a terrible realism by the apostle.

It is unnecessary for us to touch the details of the picture. It is enough to draw attention to the fact which he emphasises at the close--that the sins of which he speaks were pronounced to be sins even by the higher sense of those who practised them. The idea of divine law was not utterly gone in the Gentile mind, even amidst the sinful excesses which he describes. There was a divine voice made itself heard through all, passing judgment on such things; and the worst that could be said of the Gentiles--their deepest sin--was that they, "knowing the judgment of God, that they which commit such things are worthy of death, not only do the same, but have pleasure in them that do them." [143]

But were the Jews any better in reality? Were they any less sinners, notwithstanding all their privileges? With them there could be no question of a knowledge of the Divine. They had received the law and the prophets. The life of divine righteousness had been set forth in word, example, sacrifice, and precept, in their sacred books. To them had been committed "the oracles of God." [144] What was the outcome of all this? Much good, no doubt. This is not denied; on the contrary, it is plainly implied by the apostle. But was the life of righteousness, after all, really more conspicuous amongst them? They boasted of their privileges. They were ready and zealous in their condemnation of the heathen. But their condemnation of the heathen, the apostle states broadly, meant their own condemnation. The Jewish critic was condemned out of his own mouth,--"For wherein thou judgest another, thou condemnest thyself; for thou that judgest doest the same things." And the judgment of God is equally true against all evil-doers. It allows no one to escape. [145] Divine righteousness is impartial, and renders "to every man according to his deeds." [146] The apostle enters into an elaborate expostulation with the Jew, proving at length to him that his law of which he boasts cannot benefit him unless he has fulfilled it. For it was not the hearer but the doer of the law that was righteous before God. The Gentiles who had done what was right according to their light--who, having not the law, "had done by nature the things contained in the law," [147] were better really than the Jews, who, having their law and resting in it--knowing the divine will, and approving "the things that are more excellent, being instructed out of the law"--yet failed of its fulfilment. Of their failure in word and deed he leaves no doubt. "For the name of God is blasphemed among the Gentiles," he adds, "through you." [148] The privileges of the Jew, therefore, were nothing without the spiritual realities they were designed to represent. "For he is not a Jew who is one outwardly; neither is that circumcision which is outward in the flesh: but he is a Jew who is one inwardly; and circumcision is that of the heart, in the spirit, and not in the letter." [149]

The result of his analysis and argument is, that the Jew, merely as Jew, or an external member of the theocracy is no better than the Gentile. Both are "proved" by him to be alike "under sin." [150] The demands of divine righteousness being set over against human life, it is seen to fall infinitely below these demands. The divine ideal which encompasses it, and within which alone it can reach its true happiness, is nowhere realised. The voice of reason and conscience is quenched amongst the heathen. The law is broken by the Jew while he yet boasts of it. And what is true of Jew and Gentile, is true of man universally. The conclusion of the apostle--based upon facts of observation around him, in the Jewish and Gentile world--is plainly a conclusion of universal experience: "For all have sinned, and come short of the glory of God." [151]

2. Having thus established the universality of sin as a fact of experience, the' apostle enters upon an analysis of its character and origin in human nature. It is not enough for him to assert the fact, as the basis of his great doctrine of righteousness--not by works, but by faith. He shows how the fact originates in the constitution of human nature. There is in all men, he explains, a higher and lower

nature. The latter he everywhere designates by the term "flesh," [152] and develops its nature and properties now in antagonism to the "spirit" [153] or divine principle, and now in contrast to what he calls the "mind;" [154] for St. Paul is curiously elaborate in his analysis of human nature. He was a spiritual psychologist long before the birth of psychology as a science. The seat of sin, he says, is in the "flesh." It is the expression of this lower element of human life: "For I know that in me (that is, in my flesh) dwelleth no good thing." [155] The unregenerate "walk after the flesh;" the regenerate, "after the spirit." These two elements--the flesh and the spirit--mark the extreme poles of his thought. The one is the seat of sin and death, the other is the seat of holiness and life. The one is human nature estranged from the Divine; the other is human nature at one with the Divine--the Divine in man, as well as the divine Power above him, which raises him to the higher sphere. These two elements are always and utterly at variance. "The flesh lusteth against the spirit, and the spirit against the flesh: and these are contrary the one to the other." [156] The works of the flesh are all works of sin, as catalogued in the fifth chapter of Galatians. The fruit of the Spirit is in the higher and quite distinct sphere of the spiritual life. The breadth of this contrast everywhere appears in St. Paul's epistles, and in describing it,, the expression "flesh" is used to designate all the evil activity of human nature. It describes not merely the desires of the body, the appetites and motions of our carnal frame, but all that is in us opposed to the Divine. The mind or reason may so come under the dominion of the flesh as to be virtually identical with it. The apostle, for example, speaks of being "puffed up by a fleshly mind," [157] and even of a "fleshly wisdom." [158] The flesh, therefore is not to be confounded with mere sensuality. It is sense or nature predominant in us; our whole life of activity separated from the Divine and turned against it--not merely this life on the side of sensual passion. The mind, which is actuated by sense, and ruled by its power, is equally within the lower sphere. This is what the apostle calls "the mind" or "thought of the flesh;" and this is specially declared to be hostile to God, the enemy of the Divine. [159]

But while the mind may be thus subject to the flesh, and the two make war against the Spirit or the Divine, the mind may also itself be alive and powerful, and may enter, in its own strength, into a struggle with the flesh; in other words, the higher nature of man, always depressed and often entirely controlled by the lower nature, may also assert its own rights as an antagonist of the lower nature, and strenuously resist its domination. St. Paul seems clearly to recognise the reality of this conflict no less than the other. [160] His view sometimes enlarges to the one, sometimes contracts to the other. He now looks at human nature, banded in all its energies against the Divine, and then he looks at it as the sphere of a terrible struggle betwixt the good and the evil. This appears to be the only fair interpretation of the remarkable seventh chapter of the Epistle to the Romans, although, I need hardly say, it has been differently interpreted. Here the antagonistic elements are not the "flesh " and the "spirit," but the "flesh" and something higher within the man himself--"the inward man," [161] "the law of the mind;"[162] and the whole picture conveys the idea of the essential war there is in every conscious moral life betwixt the higher and lower principles at work within it. The general result of the apostle's analysis seems to be as follows:--

Man is a creature of mingled impulses, some higher and some lower. Moral life only begins in him with the consciousness of this double or contradictory nature, partly drawing him to good and partly drawing him to evil. It seems plainly recognised that man may go on without any moral consciousness. He may be dead in sin. [163] The flesh may usurp his whole nature. There may be nothing beyond its life in him. Conscience may be asleep, or may never lift its eyes to take in the solemn realities of duty. But it is always there, even when slumbering at its post; and when the sense of duty--or, in other words, the law--is brought home to it, there is no more contentedness in the mere natural or selfish life. The higher being is awakened. The sense of sin--previously unknown, because the sense of duty was unfelt--comes forth in full vividness against the law made clear in conscience. It requires the consciousness of the law to reveal sin in us: not that the law itself is evil, or the cause of sin; on the contrary, it is "holy, and the commandment holy, and just, and good." [164] But the revelation of the law within us, or the law consciously realised, is at the same time the revelation of sin. When the moral Ideal which should lead our lives rises clearly in the horizon of consciousness, then for the first time we feel how miserably short we come of the Ideal. It is easy to live contentedly if we have no Ideal. If we have no higher thoughts, how should our lower thoughts distract us? There is nothing for them to disturb--no higher expectations for them to clash with.

It may seem to some--it has seemed to many--a good thing to have no sense of sin. There are people who say they cannot tell what sin is; they are not conscious of it, and they may count themselves happy in this unconsciousness. Not so the apostle. There was great misery to him in the consciousness of sin; but there was something still more dreadful in its unconsciousness. This was to have sunk out of the sphere of moral experience altogether, into a mere animal or fleshly sphere; to have lost not merely the Divine, but, so to speak, the capacity of it--any trace of it upon which the higher power could take hold, and draw the sinner to itself. This was the worst of all states to him--a state in which he had found himself when "without the law sin was dead." [165] The state into which the law brought him was miserable enough, but its misery was better than insensibility. Better to feel the wretchedness of having come short of a moral Ideal, than not to have such an Ideal at all. It was true that the revelation of the law within him destroyed his self-complacency. It depressed and killed his former self-righteous life. "For I was alive," he says, "without the law once; but when the commandment came, sin revived, and I died." [166] He "had not known lust, except the law had said, Thou shalt not covet." [167] This might seem to be the worst state, and to make the law the source of sin. But not so. The sin is in human nature all the while; only the law wakes it by its quickening touch. It is as if a man were to take a candle into some noisome place full of unclean life lying torpid in the darkness, and under the searching light the life began to stir and show itself in its dark reality. Such is the effect of the law within the human heart. It makes sin manifest as a real and conscious power. And so the apostle says of it, in language that sounds paradoxical and has given rise to much controversy, but which has a real meaning to all spiritual minds like his own, that "the strength of sin is the law." [168] It is the consciousness of law that gives all its force to the consciousness of sin. And the more the law is realised as the true bond of our lives, the more fatal will its infractions be felt as they appear in these lives. The consciousness of sin, therefore, is the result of the law; but we do not infer from this, as some have done, that the apostle identifies sin and its consciousness, so that "where there is no consciousness of sin there is no sin."[169] Nothing can be further from this standpoint, as we have seen. Sin is always in human nature. It may be torpid; the flesh may have invaded the whole sphere of human activity, and killed every higher element of life. The stillness of death may reign within the darkened chamber. But this state is worse than the other, and the misery of struggle is better than the contentment of death.

The struggle which the apostle draws betwixt the higher and the lower nature is certainly a terrible one. There are not merely two elements at war within the soul, but two habits or tendencies. The flesh is not merely a succession of rebellious instincts, but "a law of sin in the members"--"a body of death."[170] The instincts of evil are gathered into an order which arrays itself against the higher order of the mind. The man is rent, as it were, in twain. His very personality is broken up--now on the side of the good, and now helpless under the evil. "It is no more I that do it, but sin that dwelleth in me. . . . For the good that I would I do not: but the evil which I would not, that I do.... I find then a law, that, when I would do good, evil is present with me. For I delight in the law of God after the inward man; but I see another law in my members, warring against the law of my mind, and bringing me into captivity to the law of sin which is in my members." [171] The language of the apostle implies the hopelessness of this struggle, looked at from a mere human point of view, so long as only the mind or the higher principle within us is the antagonist of the flesh. It must be reinforced by the Divine. The mind must be changed into the spirit,--in other words, the reason must be spiritualised. The divine Power must become ours before the power of the flesh can be mastered. Otherwise the higher self still goes down under the force of the lower--even when it clings to its Ideal, and says in despair--It is not I, but sin. "When I would do good, evil is present with me. . . O wretched man that I am! who shall deliver me from the body of this death?"

To sum up our exposition, the seat of sin we have seen with St. Paul is the "flesh." This in its broadest sense is distinguished from the "spirit." As thus distinguished, the flesh represents the whole of human nature in its estrangement from the Divine--all the activities of body and mind with which fallen man is capable of opposing the Divine. Reason, or our higher nature, may in this sense be flesh no less than the body. There may be a wisdom after the flesh and a righteousness of the same character. The idea of the flesh, in short, may invade the whole sphere of human nature, and is supposed to do so when it is brought into contact with the spirit. But the "mind," reason, or higher thought, may also set itself against the flesh, instead of yielding to the lower principle, and may enter into conflict with it in its own strength, and fight it with its native weapons. This it does more or less in all higher natures. The law of the mind refuses to bend to the law of the members, but wars against it. Unless reinforced by a higher principle it wars unsuccessfully. But this is no reason for denying the reality of the struggle, or for making human nature worse than it is. It is something that the mind refuses to bend to the flesh, and that even if beaten in the struggle, it is there to show that man has not utterly sunk into evil and made it his good.

3. We turn, in conclusion, to consider the effects or consequences of sin as described by St. Paul. These occupy a prominent place in his system of thought, and constitute an essential element of his doctrine. The effects of sin are viewed by the apostle under two aspects--the one in the main subjective, the other objective. The general name by which he describes the former is "death." "The wages of sin," he says, "is death." [172] "What fruit had ye then in those things whereof ye are now ashamed? for the end of those things is death." [173] "When we were in the flesh, the motions of sins, which were by the law, did work in our members to bring forth fruit unto death." [174] This solemn expression occurs incessantly in St. Paul's writings in connection with our subject. Death everywhere follows sin as its shadow. A state of sin is a state of death. The unregenerate are described as "dead in their sins," [175] as "dead in trespasses and sins." [176] The presence of the flesh oppressing the mind is a "body of death."[177] The issue of sin is death. It is the end to which it leads, the wages which it receives. The one cleaves to the other inseparably--not only death to sin, but sin to death. For "the sting," or "goad," "of death is sin." [178] It is

sin that urges death on, and makes it so bitter in the result.

Such language necessarily carries us, as it carried St. Paul, back to the idea of death associated with the primal sin. "Ye shall not eat of it" ("the fruit of the tree in the midst of the garden"), "neither shall ye touch it, lest ye die." [179] There the main meaning, as we formerly said, must be supposed to be spiritual. The act was a moral act. It bore with it the seeds of moral injury. Disobedience of the divine command involved the loss of that divine communion which is the true life of the moral creature. The will which had turned away from God had the seeds of weakness and wickedness implanted in it. It lost spiritual healthfulness; it sank into decay and dissolution.

But what of physical death? it may be asked. Is not this also in Scripture immediately connected with sin as its consequence? Is it not so specially in St. Paul's Epistles? [180] What, then, are we to make of this? To the modern mind death is a purely natural fact. It comes in course of time as the natural issue of all organism, which by its very life spends itself, and hastens towards dissolution as an inevitable end. We cannot conceive any individual life perpetuated under the existing laws of the external world. Continued life is only possible through death; and new organisms can only spring from the decay of the old. The physical fact of death, therefore, cannot be traced to sin as its sole cause. Nor can St. Paul be said to do this. Even when he speaks of death as the dissolution of the body, it is not only this dissolution that he means, but death with all its adjuncts of pain and sadness and spiritual apprehension. This is the death of which sin is the sting. This is the ordinary fact to all thoughtful men--not the mere decay of an organism which, because it is an organism, must decay, and by the mere fact of its living waste away. In such decay there is sadness as in all decay, yet nothing strange or gloomy. Death is always more than this to men and women who have loved and thought--all whose being has been steeped in spiritual association and passion. The natural fact is to them inseparable from its moral accessories of loss and misery. And the feeling is irresistible which associates death with all our other evil, and makes it seem, in all its painful accidents, if not in its mere occurrence, as the consequence of sin. Were there no darkness in our lives--did sin not waste and ruin them--then death could hardly be to us what it is. There would be no terror in it. The gloom of it would vanish or be less oppressive. It is this full meaning of the fact, even on its physical side for moral creatures, that the apostle brings into causal connection with sin. Death was what it was to him and his fellow-Christians because of sin. The final shadow rested on human life because that life had turned itself away from God, and chosen the evil rather than the good.

But if the apostle's view of the consequences of sin included death as an external fact, the special meaning of the fact for him as for the older Scripture writers was spiritual. It was the spiritual which included the literal, and gave its deepest stamp to the word, and not the reverse. The expressions we have already quoted plainly indicate this. The state of death which comes from sin as its immediate consequence, was the state of those living around him. It had been the state of the Ephesian and Colossian brethren previous to their conversion. It was so far the consciousness of all in whom the power of the flesh was striving successfully against the law of the mind, and bringing it into captivity to the law of sin which is in the members. [181] Conceived in this spiritual sense, death may be a passive or active state. To be dead in sin is to be as yet in the mere natural fleshly state in which the higher life has not emerged, or the law been revealed--the state to which we formerly adverted as the worst of all in the apostle's view, without God and without hope in the world. This is spiritual death in its extreme form, in which the moral nature has been so injured, depressed, and weakened, that it is not conscious of its injury. It is not there at all, in fact. The flesh has destroyed it. The lower nature has not only beaten down the higher nature, but so to speak dispossessed it, and reigns alone. There is no struggle, therefore; all is stillness, but it is the stillness of death. The true nature of the man, his moral activity, has been killed. He is therefore appropriately described as "dead in sin."

But the state of conscious struggle which is also depicted by the apostle, in which the higher nature is alive yet ineffectually active in its conflict with the flesh, is also "death." The apostle felt it to be so in his own case.. For he says, when the idea of good first came to him in the commandment, sin revived, and he died. "Who shall deliver me," he cried, "from the body of this death?" [182] The more sin is active or living within us, the more we are dead. And if we are not utterly dead, if the moral life is not gone in us altogether, but we are conscious of a good at which we ought to aim--a law which demands our service--we shall have a corresponding consciousness of fatal failure. We shall realise our own moral prostration. We shall feel, in other words, how far we have sunk from the ideal of our lives, and lost the good we ought to have had, and laid up for ourselves misery that we might have escaped,-- "wrath against the day of wrath, and revelation of the righteous judgment of God." All this experience is death to a soul in which there still live any higher thoughts. Who has not known such terrible moments-- when we have been made to possess our sins, and the iniquities of youth have laid hold of us with the grip of death; when the consciousness of lost opportunities, and enfeebled or wasted power, and the dreams of vanished good have haunted us--and we have dwelt in darkness, as them that have been long dead? Ah, my friends! these are realities, let men theorise about sin as they may. What men or women that you would care to know have not felt something of them--have not, in short, felt the sentence of death in themselves, as they have thought of what they might have done, or what they might have been, if they had striven more steadfastly, and sought the strength of God more carefully?

This brings us to the last view of St. Paul's doctrine. Death, in so far as it is spiritual, is subjective. It is a state, that is to say, in man, whether realised by him or not, But the word seems also sometimes to point to the objective relation which all sin bears to God, as when it is said that death, or a state of condemnation, "has passed upon all men, for that all have sinned." [183] In any case, such an objective relation of sin to the divine Holiness and Justice is clearly expressed in the Pauline Epistles. And the special name given to it is sufficiently emphatic. It is called the "wrath of God." [184] "The wrath of God is revealed from heaven against all ungodliness and unrighteousness of men." "Wrath against the day of wrath." [185] "Because of these things cometh the wrath of God upon the children of disobedience." [186] "Among whom also we all had our conversation in times past, in the lusts of our flesh, fulfilling the desires of the flesh and of the mind; and were by nature the children of wrath, even as others." [187] These and many other passages speak of our sin as not merely misery to ourselves, but as offensive to God, and the object of His judicial punishment. This is the special idea conveyed--disobedience in us necessarily provokes judgment in God. There can be no other relation between human sin and divine righteousness but one of condemnation--of vindictive punishment, using the words in their proper sense. This is a true element of the Pauline doctrine, and, indeed, enters into the very heart of it. Sin is not only death in us, but deserves the sentence of death. It is under the divine wrath and curse. And it would be ill with us if it were not so. If God were not sure to punish the evil, and to make it bear, so far as it remains evil, the weight of His condemnation, the good would lose for us its reality: Punishment may be hard, but it lies not only in the nature of sin itself, but in the nature of a holy divine Will that loves righteousness and hates wickedness. [188] Such a Will can only go forth towards sin in punishment of some kind, and a righteous doom must rest upon it as its due award in a righteous universe. But this subject will receive fuller consideration in our next and final Lecture.

Footnotes:
    128. Psalm i. 1, 2, 6.
    129. M. Arnold, Lit. and Dogma, p. 18.
    130. Psalm cvi. 3.
    131. Isa. i. 16, 17.
    132. Psalm iv. 4, 5.
    133. Jowett's Com. on the Epistle to the Romans, p. 54.
    134. 1 Cor. ix. 9, xiv. 34; Rom. v. 13, 20; Gal. ii. 14, 16, iii. 17, 19. See [16]Appendix XVI.
    135. Rom. ii. 17.
    136. Rom. ii. 14.
    137. Hab. ii. 4; Rom. i. 17.
    138. Rom. i. 18.
    139. Rom. i. 18.
    140. Rom. i. 19, 20.
    141. Rom. i. 21-24.
    142. Rom. i. 25.
    143. Rom. i. 32.
    144. Rom. iii. 2.
    145. Rom. ii. 2, 3 et seq.
    146. Rom. ii. 6.
    147. Rom. ii. 14.
    148. Rom. ii. 24.
    149. Rom. ii. 29.
    150. Rom. iii. 9.
    151. Rom. iii. 23.
    152. Sarx;
    153. Pneuma;
    154. Nous;
    155. Rom. vii. 18.
    156. Gal. v. 17.
    157. Phusioumenos hupo tou noos tes sarkos--Col. ii. 18.
    158. En sophia sarkike.
    159. "The carnal mind" (to phronema tes sarkos) "is enmity against God"--Rom. viii. 7.
    160. See [17]Appendix XVII.--Neander's exposition of the Pauline doctrine, in his History of the Planting and Training of the Christian Church (B. vi., c. i.), where this view seems to me to be clearly vindicated.
    161. Eso anthropon--Rom. vii. 22.

162. Nomos tou noos-Rom. vii. 23.
163. Eph. ii. 1, 5.
164. Rom. vii. 12.
165. Rom. vii. 8.
166. Rom. vii. 9.
167. Rom. vii. 7.
168. 1 Cor. xv. 56.
169. Baur's St. Paul, ii. 141; Jowett's Com. on the Epistle to the Romans, p. 504, 505. See [18]Appendix XVIII.
170. Rom. vii. 23, 24.
171. Rom. vii. 17, 19, 21-23.
172. Ta opsonia tes hamartias Thanatos--Rom. vi. 23.
173. Rom. vi. 21.
174. Rom. vii. 5.
175. Col. ii. 13.
176. Eph. ii. 1.
177. Rom. vii. 24.
178. To de kentron tou thanatou he hamartia--1 Cor. xv. 56.
179. Gen. iii. 3.
180. Rom. v. 14; 1 Cor. xv. 21, 22, 55.
181. Rom. vii. 23.
182. Rom. vii. 24.
183. Rom. v. 12.
184. Orge Theou;
185. Rom. i. 18, ii. 5.
186. Eph. v. 6; Col. iii. 6.
187. Eph. ii. 3.
188. Psalm xlv. 7.

John Tulloch, D.D.

VI – ORIGINAL SIN

IN advancing to the doctrine of original sin, we are still dealing with the Epistles of St. Paul and with the doctrine of St. Paul. Our aim has been throughout to trace the growth of the idea of sin to its full consciousness in the primitive Church; and St. Paul is the last expression of this consciousness. Within the sphere of Revelation we do not reach any further development of the doctrine, although still further developments awaited it in the thought of the fifth century, and in the later thought of Protestantism. We have been so much in the habit of identifying these later modes of thought with certain passages in the Pauline Epistles, that it is difficult for us to separate them. Such passages have so long spoken with an Augustinian or Arminian voice, that we can hardly read them without catching the argumentative tone of the one or other. But such voices are the afterthought of the Church heard in controversy, and not the original voice of St. Paul. It lies in the very principle of the historic method that we should try to distinguish the original from the after thought, and, as I said before, read always forwards instead of backwards.

Deeply as St. Augustine had drunk of the spirit of St. Paul, and closely kindred as they were in intellectual and emotional nature, they were yet widely separated in time and circumstances. There is a great interval of thought betwixt the first and the fifth century, and a very changed atmosphere surrounds the African Bishop from that which surrounded the Apostle of the Gentiles. It is well for us to know how St. Augustine interpreted St. Paul. No student can probably understand the full meaning of the latter who does not know something of the former: yet Augustinianism is something quite distinct from Paulinism. It had to deal with different questions and different adversaries--with the Pelagian instead of the Pharisee--with the full-grown Manichee instead of the infant Gnostic. In the great conflict of his day, against Manichæan and Pelagian opponents alike, St. Augustine was mighty through God in the truth of St. Paul. From the great apostle he drew the strength of his convictions, and the weapons of his warfare. He developed St. Paul's thought in order to meet and confound the errors around him; and he did this with so much power, with such a living insight into the profundities of that thought, and such a genius of intellectual and spiritual authority, that he has left the impress of his theology upon the Western Church until this day--surviving alike the influence of the Reformation and the more serious disintegration of modern criticism. The Church of the West can never speak of St. Augustine in other words than those of reverence. But this is no reason why we should only read St. Paul through his interpretations. The very dominance of his influence should rather put us on our guard against doing so. St. Paul is too great a figure even to stand behind St. Augustine, and his thought in all its bearings is to be caught if possible by the theological student in its original freshness and life. It is difficult, no doubt, to do this. It cannot be done without a special training. Standing as we do at the end of a long line of controversial thought, it is hard for us to get to the beginning and unwind the line downwards. It is much easier for us to take the end as the beginning, and not trouble ourselves further. But this is to abandon Theology as a science; and in such a case we had better let it alone altogether.

In dealing further with the Pauline doctrine of sin, or with that final aspect of it which is known as the doctrine of Original Sin, it will not be possible altogether to avoid points which owe their importance to later theology--so much of this theology rises directly out of the heart of the apostle's thought. Still it will be our aim to keep here, as elsewhere, close to our subject,--to steer as clear of controversy as we can, and to fix our attention down to the living features of the Pauline theology in itself. The interest felt in these Lectures has been mainly owing, as I fancy, to the manner in which I have sought to look at the subject, and to trace the great and solemn idea with which it is concerned along the fresh lines of its development in the spiritual consciousness of the race, rather than to make it a topic for polemical argument, however well-intentioned. Controversy can never cease in Theology any more than in other subjects of inquiry; and in it, more often than in many other subjects, the thesis or the affirmative can only be clearly seen and understood in contrast with the antithesis or negative. Truth can only be made bright in the face of error. Yet theological ideas will only rise into the region of Science, and become living ideas for all reverent intellects of whatever Church, when they have been rescued by the labours of many thinkers from the atmosphere of party controversy, and set in the light of a comprehensive inquiry into all the facts of that spiritual Order which runs through human history;--in other words, when they are seen to be real growths of that spiritual consciousness which is not only inseparable from Humanity, but which is its highest manifestation in all times of healthy moral and

The Christian Doctrine of Sin
intellectual progress.

In our preceding Lecture we dealt with the doctrine of St. Paul in so far as it may be said to be a doctrine of experience. Three special points occupied us: 1st, The universality of sin; 2d, The nature or seat of sin; and 3d, Its effects or consequences. For the proof of all these points St. Paul appealed to experience. The universality of sin was no mere theory or opinion of his, enforced by his authority. He looked on the Gentile and the Jewish world alike, and saw them "guilty before God." The righteousness or spiritual good for which man was formed--his own conscience being the witness--was nowhere realised. All had sinned and come short of that glory of God, without sharing in which there could be no human blessedness. This miserable conclusion was clearly proved to him by the facts around him; and the facts were not, alas! exceptional facts, save in some darker features. Man is no less a sinner at all points of his history than in the time of St. Paul. In explanation of the rise of sin in us, and its nature, he no less appealed to experience. His whole analysis of the "flesh" and the "spirit," and again, of the "flesh" and the "mind," and of the conflict ever raging betwixt these higher and lower elements of our being, was in the main an appeal to the experience of all in whom any higher life has been awakened, who have risen from the death of the mere nature-life to the consciousness of an Ideal or a sense of duty, for which they ought to live--after which they ought to aspire. And, lastly, in speaking of the consequences of sin, he described these as more or less experienced by all who yield to the "law of sin and death" that is in their members. The end unto death is one which sinners may or may not realise in its fulness, but it is nevertheless always a reality. The wages may be deferred, or may not be consciously received; but they are paid, without stint, sooner or later. The fatal consequences may not always equally appear, but they never fail in some form or another.

So far, therefore, the doctrine of the apostle may be said to be a doctrine of experience. His analysis is an analysis of spiritual facts, verifiable by you and by me, and by all who have the same spiritual nature. The facts may be denied. The apostle was quite well aware of this. But that did not alter his estimate of their reality. He had no doubt they would approve themselves whenever the voice of conscience was heard in a man, or the power of any divine Ideal taken hold of by him. This was enough for him. The state of those who knew nothing of the facts was out of account. It was a state worse than the most bitter consciousness of sin, because it was one in which the true life of man, as distinguished from his lower or mere animal life, had not yet emerged.

1. But besides this doctrine of experience, there is a further doctrine in St. Paul--a philosophy of the subject, which in part at least transcends experience. Sin is not only in human nature--the expression of that lower side of it which he calls the "flesh,"--but it is an hereditary characteristic of it. Man is born in sin. In one sense, this may be said to be a mere truism. If man is composed of flesh as well as mind or reason--if there is a lower carnal life in all, and the only question is not as to the experience of the lower but of the higher life--then there can be no doubt that sin is an original element of human nature. It comes to us by birth. The universality of sin implies that sin is the outgrowth of original tendencies, and that man is a sinner, not merely by the fact that he deliberately chooses the evil rather than the good, but because his nature is evil, or has inherited evil properties. To this extent, the doctrine of original sin is a mere generalisation from obvious facts. The mixed impulses with which we come into the world bear their natural fruit of good and evil. Not only so; but, as it is the lower or animal side of human life that may be said to grow first--to put forth its shoots with most vigour in the beginning--it is inevitable that the manifestations of our lower life should show an early activity, and that evil rather than good should spring up in the fertile soil. There is nothing that can be said to transcend experience in such a doctrine as this; nor is there anything in it that can well admit of question on any hypothesis of human origin and destiny.

That all individual men and women are what they are of good or evil, in virtue not only of their own individual acts, but of inherited tendencies which have descended from a long antecedent past, is so far an indisputable conclusion. No creature is, so to speak, merely itself in the world. It is where it is, or what it is, as the result of an indefinite advance and appropriation of preceding forms of existence. And this is true not only of the forms of animal life, but of all organic forms, moral and intellectual as well as animal. There is a continuous growth everywhere, and all share in this growth. All come forth from the teeming bosom of the past. None stand isolated or self-centred. Not to speak of the necessary connection between the higher and the lower nature of man--a connection which none can deny, however strenuously they may resist the materialistic interpretations drawn from it--intellectual and moral life by themselves are seen to run along continuous threads, and to grow into what they are as the result of many accessories. They are no more isolated than any other phenomena of nature and of life.

The doctrine of hereditary corruption, therefore, stating it merely as we are now stating it, is so far from being contradictory to modern ideas, that it may be said to be a direct corollary from the doctrine of evolution. Assuming that there is sin at all in the world, or something answering to what we call sin, it becomes a direct inference from the scientific observation of facts, that sin has propagated itself from generation to generation and from race to race. If it is a feature in humanity, it is a feature which has come to us from our progenitors, and contributed its share to make man what he now is. If what we call corruption is universal, then it is necessarily hereditary. For, in fact, there is nothing in our human nature, or, for that part of the matter, in nature anywhere, which is not so far hereditary. All forms of life and activity have a lineage. They are only what they are as the outcome of this lineage; and man, therefore, can only be a sinner because he has come of a line of sinners, and the evil that is in him has been passed over to him from those who have gone before him.

2. But the doctrine of the apostle is something more than this: it is something, indeed, very different from this. His mind does not move on the plane of inductive observation at all. He was a great master of facts within the spiritual sphere, a psychological analyst of no mean skill. He delights to deal with the realities of our inward experience, and to make the truth manifest in the sight of conscience. But he would never have dreamt of looking for any confirmation of his special doctrine in the laws of the natural world. The natural world was far less real to him than the spiritual,--and cosmic conceptions had no place in his mind beside the religious and scholastic conceptions in which he had been bred as a Pharisee, and which were illuminated and spiritualised, not extinguished, by his Christian culture. In his full explanation of the universality of sin, therefore, he rises into a quite different atmosphere, and travels beyond the range of ordinary experience. Sin is with him not merely transmitted to us, as all our qualities must be transmitted: but it comes to us by definite passage from the sin of Adam as the prototype and representative of our race. His idea of original sin is not simply the transmission of sinful qualities from generation to generation by the principle of natural inheritance. It is an idea of spiritual injury and penal consequence inflicted upon the race by the first sin, and directly imputed to the race in consequence of that sin. This is the doctrine which he lays down in two well-known passages, [189] one of which in the fifth chapter of the Epistle to the Romans has long been a subject of difficulty and controversy.

It may be urged, as some have done, [190] that too much importance has been attached to these passages of St. Paul. They form, after all, but a small part of his writings--a few verses amongst thousands. Yet the commentary on them has filled the Christian world, and great parties in the Church have waged around them an incessant strife. It may be granted that Christian controversialists have made too much of these detached portions of St. Paul's writings. It is the bane of all controversy to concentrate attention upon single points, and to forget the connection of thought and doctrine in the emphasis of these points. Texts have played an unhappy part in the history of Theology, and led men's minds away from the balance and co-ordination of Christian truth. This has come from a wrong conception of Revelation, and is passing away with the conception out of which it sprang. But, admitting this, we may be sure that the instinct of the Church has not been wrong in attributing vital importance to the passages in question, and that they bring before us very fundamental elements of St. Paul's thought. His doctrine of original sin may have been argued too endlessly in the Church, and drawn out into conclusions which it will hardly bear. But it is one of real moment in his whole system of thought.

The passage in the Epistle to the Romans runs as follows in our version: [191] "Wherefore, as by one man sin entered into the world, and death by sin; and so death passed upon all men for that all have sinned. For until the law" (up to the time of giving the law) "sin was in the world; but sin is not imputed where there is no law. Nevertheless death reigned from Adam to Moses, even over them that had not sinned after the similitude of Adam's transgression, who is the figure of him that was to come." Further, in the nineteenth verse: [192] "As by one man's disobedience many were made sinners, so by the obedience of one shall many be made righteous." The passage in the fifteenth chapter of the First Epistle to the Corinthians is comparatively brief and general: "For as in Adam all die, even so in Christ shall all be made alive." [193]

The thought of the apostle in these and other passages circulates around Adam on the one hand, and Christ on the other, as centres of spiritual influence. The state of man before Christ, and the state of man after--or of all who belong to Christ and share in His redeeming work--is strongly contrasted. Adam, as sinner, gives its character to the one; Christ, as Saviour and the righteous One, gives its character to the other. In the passage from the Epistle to the Romans, sin and death are represented as the ruling powers in the world. Adam is the source through which they have entered into the world. Through his one act of sin, Adam not only fell himself, but the line of spiritual integrity was broken in him. The flaw extended to the race. "Sin entered into the world, and death by sin; and so death passed upon all, for that all have sinned." In other- words, sin passed to us from Adam, and death from sin. This is the simple meaning of the words as they stand in our version. They might seem at first to add little to the doctrine of hereditary corruption as generalised from the facts of experience. But on a closer view they will be found to add various features to this doctrine. They emphasise the position of Adam as not merely the first in a line of sinners, but as the type or representative of the whole line--one whose act was fatal not only for himself, but for all who followed him. All mankind fell with him into the death which he had incurred. (a.) This typical character of Adam; (b.) the descent of spiritual depravity from him; and (c.) the fatal character of the results which followed not only for himself but for his posterity--in other words, the judicial character of these results in their downward passage--are all ideas more or less involved in the passage. Let us look at them a little more carefully, and see how far they are true ideas of the apostle without special reference to the deductions of later theology.

(a.) As to the first or the typical character of Adam, there can be no doubt. This thought is plainly implied in the passage as a whole, as well as in the passage quoted from the fifteenth chapter of the First Epistle to the Corinthians, and in other passages of the same chapter. [194] It is a familiar thought of the apostle. Adam was with him not only the first man historically, but the first man representatively. He stands before all others not only in time, but in idea. He is the earthly type, as Christ is the spiritual type, of humanity. This contrast of typical relation is no accident of the apostle's thought. It is embedded in it, and reappears constantly. There is a sense to him in which mankind were summed up in Adam, as believers are summed up in Christ. He has a profound feeling of the unity of the race, and of this unity Adam is a type or symbol. His act is therefore more than his own act. It has consequences not merely of historical sequence, but of representative meaning.

(b.) But the unity of the human race is with St. Paul no mere natural unity, or unity of external conditions. He looks at man not from the outside, but from the inside, and sees the race everywhere bound together by inward links. It is true that it is the lower and not the higher side of humanity that Adam represents and sums up. Christ is the representative of the higher or spiritual side--the Lord from heaven. But even man's lower relations are inwardly apprehended. It is not merely natural dispositions that have come from Adam--it is sin--an inward depravity--a will enfeebled for all that is good, and prone to all that is evil. This inward view of the apostle separates his thought from all mere physiological considerations. These he neither denied nor affirmed. They were out of his sight. When he speaks of man, even on the lower or earthly side of his being, as represented by Adam,--he thinks of him as a being under moral conditions and responsibilities. The transmission of sin, therefore, is with him not a mere accumulation of evil dispositions and tendencies, but an injury in the will or moral power.

(c.) This injury is characterised by him as death. In our last Lecture we so far expounded the meaning of this expression, and promised to return to it; and it is in connection with this subject, or the consequences of Adam's sin, that the special difficulty of St. Paul's doctrine arises. The full force of what the apostle means by death is brought before us in the two passages under consideration. It is the dissolution of the inward life of righteousness, which is alone the true life of all the true children of God. But it is also more than this. It is a state of condemnation, or of liability to punishment. The presence of sin is not merely ruinous in us, but it calls down the judgment of God. The "wrath of God is revealed from heaven against all ungodliness and unrighteousness of men." There can be no other relation betwixt our unrighteousness and the righteousness of God but a relation of condemnation. And this relation is passed over to men by the Fall. "And so death has passed upon all men, for that" (eph' ho) "all have sinned."

The precise meaning of these few words has been vehemently contested. Do they imply merely, as in our version is all their obvious meaning, that as death followed the sin of Adam, so death follows the sin of all? All die, because all have sinned. Or is the thought that death or condemnation follows directly and universally the commission of Adam's sin, irrespective of personal sin? Under the influence of this last view Augustine translated the words, "in whom all have sinned;" and this translation has passed into the Vulgate. [195] Instead of translating the words conjunctively, as from the earlier times of the Church they had been understood, and as they are rendered in our version, he sought to find a subject to the relative [196] in Adam as the first man. But no modern scholar can be said to advocate this translation, which, moreover, yields a meaning at variance with the context. For how does the apostle proceed in his argument? "For until the law," he says, or up to the time of the law, "sin was in the world; but sin is not imputed when there is no law." He had stated that sin was introduced into the world by one man, or by Adam's transgression of the divine law, and that death had followed sin, and passed upon all. But an objection seems to occur to him--If sin is always the transgression of law, what are we to make of the period betwixt Adam and Moses, when there was no positive law given to mankind? How could sin be reckoned against man when there was no law? He answers in the verses that follow: "Nevertheless death reigned from Adam to Moses, even over them that had not sinned after the similitude of Adam's transgression." The evidence, therefore, that there was really sin in the world then, is that death prevailed. It is true that sinners then were not sinners in the same sense as Adam. They did not transgress a positive divine law as he did. But they were none the less sinners. Although they had no definite law or express divine command given them to test their obedience, they had the law of reason and of conscience. The voice of God might have been heard in their hearts if they had listened to it. But they failed to do this, and they sinned therefore, although not after the similitude of Adam's sin. He does not explain all this. His reasoning is enigmatic here, as in many other places; but this is clearly his thought, as elsewhere expressed in the epistle. The sufficient evidence to his mind of the presence of sin in all the time from Adam to Moses is the prevalence of death during this time. Death reigned then as at other times.

It seems plain, therefore, that the apostle connects death in every case with the personal commission of sin. The death which has passed upon all men is not merely a death on account of Adam's sin, but on account of their own sins. Death is everywhere the evidence of sin. It implies sin; and its universality, therefore, is a proof of the universality of sin, just as its prevalence during the period from Adam to Moses was a proof that men were sinners then as at all other times, although they were not living under definite law. "The apostle's idea is, that sin as well as death is universal, and that they are inseparably linked to each other. The universality of sin, however, is not so immediately and clearly apparent as the universality of death; and so it is inferred that sin is universal from the fact that death is universal, there being no death apart from sin, which is its cause. The whole argument shows distinctly that, though he sees in sin and death the operation of a principle reigning in humanity since Adam, he yet conceives the death of man to be essentially connected with his own sin: Death came to all,' or passed upon all, because all have sinned.' The coming of death, in other words, cannot be explained except on the supposition that all have sinned. The one always involves the other." [197]

While on the one hand, therefore, death follows from Adam's sin, it is no less inseparably connected in every case with personal sin. In other words, while the punishment of Adam's sin did not stay with himself, but was diffused with the diffusion of the sin which he initiated, it is not passed over by itself merely. The true relation is--(1) Adam's sin; (2) Our sin; (3) Death cleaving necessarily to both. But it may be said, Does not the death of infants, who commit no actual sin, and who are yet subject to death, imply the imputation of Adam's sin to them? If death and sin are inseparable, is not their death to be explained only by the fact that Adam's sin and death are passed over to them? Whatever force there may be in such a view, it certainly derives no confirmation from the present passage, which distinctly asserts the personal presence of sin as the cause or explanation of death. But what, then, of the death of infants? This, which was a puzzle in the fifth century, cannot, in the same degree, puzzle us, for reasons I have more than once explained. The dissolution of the physical system is nowhere in St. Paul nor in Scripture represented as solely the result of sin. The death of Adam, the death of sin, in St. Paul, is always something more than mere physical death. It may include the death of the body--it does this plainly and prominently in the passage before us--but it always includes more; and, even when it refers to physical death, it is not the decay of nature--the extinction of an organism, which is the essential note of the word--but the pain and misery and spiritual apprehension which the decay, in the case of human beings, irresistibly suggests. It is beyond doubt that death itself, in the mere sense of decay, is inherent in all organism; that the conditions of life, in short, are death; and that infant organic structures consequently should die when weak, or imperfect, or ready to vanish away, is no more remarkable than that any other organism should perish. The mystery of all life and death when we go beneath the surface, as we are incessantly prompted to do in the case of human beings, is impenetrable. But on the surface there is no more mystery in one case than another. Death follows the exhaustion of living tissue in young and old alike, and, as a mere natural fact, is independent of moral conditions, or, at least, nowhere solely follows them.

The physical death of infants, therefore, does not require sin to explain it. And as to anything further, we have no knowledge. The final fate of infants, which perplexed Augustine's mind, cannot perplex ours. Of the meaning of death in the future, or what is known as perdition, we have no call here to speak. The reality that is in it comes from sin; it is the final punishment of sin. And those who go down in darkness to dwell in misery outside the Divine presence are receiving in the end wages due to them. The thought is awful enough, and may well make sinners pause before their feet stumble, and the light pass from their eyes, and, behold, there is only darkness. But it would not only be awful, but horrible, if we supposed that this dread reality awaited any life which had not here come to moral consciousness, or known the choice of good and evil. If we can be sure of anything at all, we may be sure of this, that God will deal with all as they have really done, rendering unto every man according to his works. If there is any moral truth at all, this is moral truth--that God will act fairly, and that none will receive what they have not deserved in their own doings. There is no principle more frequently enunciated both in the New and the Old Testament Scriptures. Whatever, therefore, may be the consequence of Adam's sin to infants, we may be sure that they will not suffer for these consequences. As they have not known to do evil, they cannot have evil rendered to them. Their fate may be beyond our scrutiny. An impenetrable veil may rest upon it, and we may never be able to lift it; but we take refuge in the sure truth, that the Judge of all will do what is right, and that He to whom we commit the child-life, which He has mysteriously given and mysteriously taken away, is "our Father which art in heaven"--whose face the angels of little children continually behold. [198]

But what, then, is the precise force of our relation to Adam? To what extent do we suffer for his sin? What is imputed to us in consequence? The death which is passed upon all men--what is it more particularly? We have already seen that the relation of Adam to the sinful race which has proceeded from him is typical. There is more in it to his posterity than there in the relation of any other man to the race; and this not merely because he was first in natural order, but because the race was in a certain sense anticipated in him or summed up in him. It admits of no doubt that this was one of the governing ideas of the apostle's mind. Whether we make it any more clear by drawing it out according to our own imperfect analogies, and turning the mystery into a logical illustration, seems questionable. But plainly it was in the mind of the apostle that we suffer directly from Adam's sin--not merely in the loss of spiritual faculty and divine good which we would otherwise have possessed--but in definite punishment. God deals with the race judicially on account of it, as a sinful race. As our Confession of Faith' has it, (Our first parents being the root of all mankind, the guilt of their sin was imputed, and the same death, and sin, and corrupted nature conveyed to all their posterity." [199] I am glad to be able to quote these words for their own sake, and because of their source. They are weighty and, upon the whole, sober words; and although they necessarily take us away from the immediate atmosphere of Scripture, they do not seem to me, rightly understood, to exceed the fair meaning of St. Paul.

The terms of the statement in the Confession are deserving of particular attention. They speak not of an imputation of sin--as many have done unadvisedly--but of the guilt of sin. And the distinction is an important one in theological language. The expression "guilt" has always had more meanings than one, and the theological language of the sixteenth and seventeenth centuries is only intelligible when this is kept in view. When we say that a man is guilty, we primarily mean that he has really done the crime or evil deed imputed to him. But when a person is pronounced guilty, or has incurred guilt, we also mean that he has become obnoxious to punishment. Here, as often elsewhere, the meaning of a familiar word runs out into a secondary and even a tertiary sense. First, and properly, the word means personal ill-doing. If I say to myself, "I am guilty," I accuse myself of a wrong that I ought not to have done. The idea is specially and prominently that of self-reference. The evil I could not, or should not, I have done. But the idea is also that of self-condemnation, or the desert of punishment. I deserve to suffer for what I have done. The two feelings are inseparable. Conscious wrong-doing is at the same time conscious condemnation. And every wrong-doer who has been brought to a sense of his wrong will have the one feeling as well as the other. And even if the wrongdoer have no sense of his wrong, the fact that he has committed a wrong, and that he deserves punishment for it, is not altered in his case. Let the act be carried home to him, and let it be proved that he did it--that he was, as it is said, art and part in it--and he only deserves punishment all the more that he has professed unconsciousness of the act, or added falsehood to his folly or crime. In these two meanings the proper or the moral sense of guilt is summed up; and it would have been better, therefore, that the use of the word had not been extended further. But it has been extended in theological language to the still further or tertiary sense of liability to punishment as the consequence of wrong-doing. The results of wrong accumulate and descend, not only upon the offender, but upon all connected with him. And the term "guilt" has been passed over to denote this condemned state, or state of punishment.

This is the only intelligible sense in which it can be said that the guilt of Adam's sin is imputed to us.[See [19]Appendix XXI.] We did not personally participate in Adam's sin. We cannot be brought to feel that we did so, or that we deserve punishment for having done so. The race may deserve punishment inasmuch as it was summed up in him as its representative, and that in this sense it sinned and fell in him. There are those who think that the apostle's meaning is not exhausted without this deeper view of this subject which takes in the whole of humanity as bound up in Adam--as a united whole in him, and dealt with as a whole. His ill-deserving is therefore passed over to all, although in the nature of things, or on the broad ground of natural reason, that personal merit or demerit is incommunicable, it can never be brought home to all. It must be admitted that the apostle's language is of a strongly realistic turn, and that he conceives Adam and his race as, so to speak, identified in the divine view. This has been clearly allowed in our exposition; but it has been equally clear that sin itself, and the ill-desert that comes from it, as always personal, are not imputable. If this extreme view, therefore, be maintained, it can only be as a mystery--as something lying behind the region of ordinary thought. The clear dictate of conscience is, that we can only deserve ill when we have done ill.

No one more clearly recognises this axiom of the moral sense than the apostle himself. In the very passage which has been more or less the basis of all our thought in this Lecture, we have seen how clearly he brings out death as always the consequence of personal sin, and not merely of Adam's sin. The personal element is always emphasised by him, as by all the Biblical writers, in connection with sin. It is you and I who sin, and who will be punished for our own sins. This broad moral commonplace, intelligible by all, owned by all, runs through Scripture, and is the great line upon which all its exhortations and warnings turn. It seems hardly possible to attach the conception of ill-desert to anything but personal wrong-doing. It may be doubted if the apostle ever intends to do this, realistic as is his conception of humanity, and of the relation in which it stands to the first man.

But neither can there be any doubt that he passes over to humanity the state of condemnation or obnoxiousness to punishment into which Adam fell. That is to him a matter of fact. Adam's sin is in this sense guilt to all, that it brings punishment to all. And if there is also mystery in this,--that a race should be punished because the first man kept not his first estate--if the moral sense is not without difficulty here (there may be those who think the difficulty hardly a step removed),--there are at least also broad facts of experience that come in to help us in facing this mystery. It is a fact, however we may explain it, that guilt in this sense is imputable. The punishment of wrong-doing descends far beyond the wrongdoer. Children are involved in their parents' shame. A family without any ill-deserving suffers many ills, and even a sort of death itself, from the criminality of its head. A nation is plunged into misery, and reaps the reward of iniquity through all its bounds, when its chief men stand condemned at the bar of moral judgment, or have plunged it into flagrant wrong. If it be true that sin is' always personal, and God will render unto every man according to his works, it is no less true that all sin is diffusive, and carries with it a train of endless consequences, many of them of a strictly penal character. We may be sure we will not suffer at last for anything that we have not done. In point of fact, the question is a theoretical one for all who have grown to know good and evil. "If we say that we have no sin, we deceive ourselves, and the truth is not in us."[200] From the first dawn of moral consciousness, we have been conscious of short-coming. Actual sin has become inextricably interwoven in us with original sin, and we stand on our own deserts before the bar of divine judgment. We need not therefore trouble ourselves with the question how far we shall be punished for the sins of another, seeing our own sins are more than can be reckoned up, and that we know in our hearts, if we know anything, that no injustice will be done us by Him who judges righteously.

It was necessary, all the same, that this deeper view of the subject should come before us, and that we should look at the question of sin not merely on its personal, but, so to speak, its impersonal or original side. Both sides must be taken together. If we look at human nature merely in its historic connection, we seem bound in a chain of external facts, which leaves no room for personal freedom. The very idea of sin seems to vanish in its necessity. How can man be blamable for what he cannot help--for that which is the mere outcome of the nature which God has given him? If God has so connected us with a sinful race, and so connected the race with its fallen original,--then all seems His own doing. And having made us what we are,. how can He punish us that we are no better than we are? If we push the doctrine of original sin as some have done, we end in the subversion of sin altogether. But we look within, and we know that, whatever may be our connection with a given order of events which hold us in their dependence, we are free to act--that if we sin daily, we yet can help sinning--that even when temptation is at its strongest we can turn away from it, and choose that which is right and good. Nay, we know that the Right and Good form the true law of our being, to which we are truly bound, and not the wrong or the evil which yet so often bind us. There is that in us which is, deeper than all sinful habit, and which no force of original sin can overcome, if only we give it free play. And if we do not do so,--if we yield to the lower rather than to the higher--to the evil rather than to the good,--we know that we deserve to receive evil, and that punishment is our due. All our experience is thus mixed. We are bound, and yet we are free; we are sharers in original sin, and yet we ourselves are sinners; inheritors of evil, and yet voluntarily evil-doers. We may be unable to coordinate the two sides of our experience, but this is no reason why we should not acknowledge the one side as well as the other.

If we start merely from a single side of human nature, it is easy to build up systems, and there are minds which will always demand such systems. The Theological Necessitarian has had his day in the past; and, blind to the discrimination of moral facts, he has drawn out his theory till it has covered the whole field of Christian thought. It is now the high day of the Materialistic Necessitarian, who is prepared to explain all life--intellectual and moral as well as physical--from microscopic germs up to its most subtle and lofty developments. Such systems are said to be rigorous and consistent, and to know what they are about. They do not palter in a double sense, or stand with trembling and agitated gaze on the brink of mystery. All haze has gone from them; almighty Power in the one case, and almighty Law in the other, is made to solve all--to open the shell of the universe and show its secret. The modern system-monger seems quite as sure of this secret as the most confident theologian of the ancient school. He goes forth into the darkness with his naturalistic law of evolution in his hand, and all seems to him to fall into order. The great modern idea is to swallow up all the thought of the past, and to bear humanity prosperously into a dim future without a soul and without a God. But the facts of moral life are not thus to be borne down. They spring up irrepressibly from every attempt to merge them in some theoretic principle which only explains them at the expense of their reality. In this way they are not to be solved. They claim to be heard for themselves, and to vindicate their independence, however difficult it may be to reconcile them with any preconceived theory. The thinker, who feels bound to recognise both sides of human experience--the moral and intellectual alike--the spiritual and the scientific together,--who shrinks from no discovery of science and no advance in knowledge, and yet clings to the realities of the inner life and the verities of a Divine order,--has a hard time of it betwixt system-builders on the one side and the other;--the bigotries of an omniscient Science on the one hand, and the jealousies of an omniscient Theology on the other. He is flaunted by the one and suspected by the other. But the moderation which refuses to affirm where the grounds of affirmation are wanting, and is content to explore and recognise facts of whatever kind, even where it cannot co-ordinate them or bind them into a theory, is at once the best note of science, and the surest pledge of a theology that has some promise for the future, as well as hold upon the past.

And now I have done with these Lectures. It has been to me a grateful surprise that so many should have felt so true an interest in them. If I have said anything that has helped or may yet help any to think more truly of a great verity of our spiritual nature, or of the verities of religious life and doctrine altogether. I have reason to thank God and take courage. I have said nothing, I hope, in any case, which can serve to lessen the solemn reality of the great truth of which I have been speaking. I have endeavoured to keep close to my task of scientific exposition, and to allow as few jarring notes as possible to enter from any side. This appears to me--it has long appeared to me--the only useful mode of treating Christian doctrine.

Let us, in conclusion, remember that the sin of which I have been speaking is our own--your sin and mine; and that if there is sin at all, it is necessarily always misery. It bears its own doom with it. But the Son of God "was manifested to take away our sins, and in Him is no sin."[201] His name is Jesus, because "He saves His people from their sins."[202] He has come into the world, "not to condemn the world, but that the world through Him might be saved."[203] If we are conscious of the conflict of sin in ourselves--if in our higher moments, when we are ravished by the Good, we are yet held back by the Evil, and when we delight in the law of God, according to the inward man, we yet find a law in our members warring against the law of our minds, and bringing us into captivity to the law of sin and death--let us remember that there is One who is able to help us, and who will not suffer us to be tempted above what we are able to bear; and let our prayer be--who would not have the experience out of which such a prayer springs, bitter though it be, rather than rest in the deadness of sin?--Save us, good Lord, and bring us from all the weary and sinful struggle of this mortal life to Thine own holy peace, and Thine everlasting kingdom and glory. Amen.

Footnotes:

189. Rom. v. 12 et seq.; 1 Cor. xv. 22.
190. See remarks of Mr. Jowett, [20]Appendix XIX.
191. Dia touto hosper di' henos anthropou he hamartia eis ton kosmon eiselthen, kai dia tes hamartias ho thanatos, kai houtos eis pantas anthropous ho thanatos dielthen, eph' o pantes hemarton. Achri gar nomou hamartia en en kosmo, hamartia de ouk ellogeitai me ontos nomou. Alla ebasileusen ho thanatos apo Adam mechri Mouseos kai epi tous me hamartesantas epi to homoiomati tes parabaseos Adam, hos estin tupos tou mellontos.--Rom. v. 12-14.
192. Hosper gar dia tes parakoes tou henos anthropou hamartoloi katestathesan hoi polloi, houtos kai dia te?s hupakoe?s tou? henos dikaioi katastathesontai hoi polloi.--Rom. v. 19.
193. Hosper gar en to Adam pantes apothneskousin, houtos kai en to Christo? pantes zoopoiethesontai.--1 Cor. xv. 22.
194. 1 Cor. xv. 45, 47.
195. "In quo omnes peccaverunt." See [21]Appendix XX. for a more special statement of Augustine's views.
196. ho.
197. Baur's St. Paul, ii. 185.
198. Matt. xviii. 10, 14.
199. Westminster Confess. of Faith, c. vi. III.
200. 1 John, i. 8.
201. 1 John, iii. 5.
202. Matt. i. 2.
203. John, iii. 17.

John Tulloch, D.D.

APPENDIX

I

(Lecture I., page 8.)

THEOLOGY AND NATURAL SCIENCE.

SOME more definite passage to the effect of what I have here stated was running in my head when I wrote my Lecture. But I have failed to verify it. The tone of thought, however, which is implied in the text is not uncommon, and may be sufficiently illustrated by the following extract from one of David Hume's Essays ("Of the Academical or Sceptical Philosophy," in the Inquiry concerning the Human Understanding'), with accompanying comment by Professor Huxley. The extract and comment are found in the close of Professor Huxley's address "On the Physical Basis of Life"--Lay Sermons,' &c., p. 150:--

"If we take in hand any volume of divinity, or school metaphysics, for instance, let us ask, Does it contain any abstract reasoning concerning quantity and number? No. Does it contain any experimental reasoning concerning matter of fact and existence? No. Commit it then to the flames, for it can contain nothing but sophistry and illusions.'

"Permit me to enforce this most wise advice. Why trouble ourselves about matters of which, however important they may be, we do know nothing, and can know nothing? We live in a world which is full of misery and ignorance; and the plain duty of each and all of us is to try to make the little corner he can influence somewhat less miserable and somewhat less ignorant than it was before he entered it. To do this effectually, it is necessary to be possessed of only two beliefs: the first, that the order of nature is ascertainable by our faculties to an extent which is practically unlimited; the second, that our volition counts for something as a condition of the course of events. Each of these beliefs can be verified experimentally as often as we like to try."

Nothing else, of course, of the nature of theological truth--which neither concerns "quantity and number," nor yet in Hume's sense "matter of fact and existence"--can be verified experimentally, and why then trouble ourselves about what we can never know?

II

(Lecture I., page 10.)

KANT'S RECOGNITION OF THE MORAL LAW.

"Two things there are, which, the oftener and the more steadfastly we consider, fill the mind with an ever-new, an ever-rising admiration and reverence--the starry heaven above, the moral law within. Of neither am I compelled to seek out the reality, as veiled in darkness, or only to conjecture the possibility, as beyond the hemisphere of my knowledge. Both I contemplate lying clear before me, and connect both immediately with my consciousness of existence. The one departs from the place I occupy in the outer world of sense; expands, beyond the bounds of imagination, this connection of my body with worlds rising beyond worlds, and systems blending into systems; and protends it also into the illimitable times of their periodic movement--to its commencement and perpetuity. The other departs from my invisible self, from my personality; and represents me in a world, truly infinite indeed, but whose infinity can be tracked out only by the intellect, with which also my connection, unlike the fortuitous relation I stand in to all worlds of sense, I am compelled to recognise as universal and necessary. In the former, the first view of a countless multitude of worlds annihilates, as it were, my importance as an animal product, which, after a brief and that incomprehensible endowment with the powers of life, is compelled to refund its constituent matter to the planet--itself an atom in the universe--on which it grew. The other, on the contrary, elevates my worth as an intelligence even without limit; and this through my personality, in which the moral law reveals a faculty of life independent of my animal nature--nay, of the whole material world,--at least if it be permitted to infer as much from the regulation of my being, which a conformity with that law exacts; proposing, as it does, my moral worth for the absolute end of my activity, conceding no compromise of its imperative to a necessitation of nature, and spurning, in its infinity, the conditions and boundaries of my present transitory life."--Hamilton's Lectures on Metaphysics,' i. 39, 40. The passage is the first paragraph of the conclusion (Beschluss) of the Kritik der Praktischen Vernunft,' and will be found in vol. viii. p. 312 of Kant's 'Sämmtliche Werke' (Leipzig, 1838).

III

(Lecture I., page 13.)

MODERN SCHOOL OF DUTCH DIVINES--DE ETHISCHE RICHTING.

Holland has been during the last quarter of a century a soil even more fertile than Germany in the fruits of theological learning and speculation. The critico-historical labours of Kuenen and others are now well known in this country by all interested in such subjects; but comparatively little as yet is known of the school to which I refer in the text (spoken of in their own country as "De Modernen")-- who may be characterised as the extreme left of the theological movement presently so active in the churches and universities of Holland. The leaders of this school are Dr. Hooykaas, one of the compilers of the Bible for Young People,' and an able young theologian of the name of Van Hamel, who has sustained in the press the chief part in defending and developing the views of the Ethical Theory of Religion.' I am indebted to an accomplished young clergyman in our own Church, Mr. Menzies of Abernyte, who is well versed both in German and Dutch Theology, for the following statement of the views of these writers, translated and summarised from articles which have appeared on the subject within the last two years in the Theologisch Tijdschrift.'

"Hooykaas [204] starts with saying, God is--He acts'--that is a matter of experience. But suppose we have still to seek Him, in what way are we to arrive at a knowledge of Him? Religion is a fact; but what are the contents of religion? Turning to history, we find that the gods whom men have worshipped began with being material physical powers, but have gradually come to be moral powers. Parsism, Mosaism, Christianity, the New School in Holland, each is a step in this direction. And not only so; but the moral element has been the essence of religion all along. Hence we are in sympathy with Isaiah or Augustine, though our theology is radically different from theirs.

"To us God is Holy Love. It is not His power but His love that we worship. To us there is nothing adorable in the Nature-God, the Ruler; we ourselves are superior to all power. To us the Divine is what is holy, noble, exalted--the Moral Ideal, in fact.

"The reason why religion thus proceeds from the material to the moral, from the outward power to the spiritual power, is just that the latter is the higher of the two, and that as man grows he becomes fitter to appreciate and to worship it. It is ever coming to us, this Moral Ideal, and we grow capable of answering to its appeals.

"The moral power acts. We know that to be good is better than to be bad. This is its action. Only the moral man can judge of this, however. To him who is seeking earnestly to be good, the consciousness of the reality of the moral law becomes so strong that he will rather doubt the existence of the sensible than of the moral world. Belief in the reality of moral ideas is the very essence of religion.'

"Hooykaas insists again and again on the immediateness of the knowledge of this power. It is not a conclusion drawn from certain facts; it is the fact itself.' We know God in so far as He reveals Himself to us. Of His essence, of His existence, apart from that revelation, we know nothing.' In support of this position, he refers to the unconscious suggestions of a higher life, of sympathy, of enthusiasm for righteousness, of duty, which came to good men. Not we,' he says, took the first step--the Ideal drew us to itself before we thought of it; we loved God because He first loved us. The Ideal exists; it is not developed out of humanity, but impresses itself on the consciousness of humanity. At each step in the revelation, at each advance in clear perception of the Ideal, we are aware that we are not the producers but the recipients. . . .

"Your theory of the world may be anything you choose; that is quite apart from your religion. Ultimately, indeed, your faith will mould your views on various subjects. It will be impossible for you to believe that an evil power created the world, or that the world, with all the achievements and the aspirations of millenniums, is doomed to utter extinction. Faith in a God whom you thus immediately know will also bias you in favour of an intuitive theory of morals. . . . An atheist is not a man who denies the existence of God, who rejects any particular conception of what God is, nor even a man who denies the reality of moral distinctions, and asserts that good and evil are alike the will of God, but a man who practically denies the existence and authority of moral powers, and asserts in his actions that there is no such thing as love, that self-interest is the universal and the only rule, that sensual desires have an intrinsic right to be satisfied, that money is the supreme power and lawgiver in human society. The conception of God matters very little; what is important is to have God Himself. There is no religion without God; but there is religion without any conception of God. We point to ourselves as examples of that fact.'

"Dr. Hooykaas then goes on to argue that he has a right to retain the name God and the word religion for this position, although these terms have hitherto borne a totally different significance. God, he asserts, means essentially Higher Power, and more definitely an Invisible Supreme Power, which claims and is worthy of our adoration; and in this sense he can use the old word without any reserve of the Moral Ideal by which good men are visited and the human race drawn upwards. He enters then on a demonstration that this conception of God is the key to a proper understanding of the Jewish prophets and of Jesus. In this we need scarcely follow him, as we are all familiar with an argument which is essentially the same. Dr. Hooykaas' demonstration differs from Dr. Matthew Arnold's in this, that the righteous power--Dr. Arnold would say which, Dr. Hooykaas says whom--the prophets and Jesus more and more vividly apprehended is with the Dutchman a living, moving power, drawing near to the spirits of those who were fit to know Him."

The writer who has gone furthest of all in the identification of true religion with morality is Van Hamel, [205] who has published in the Theologisch Tijdschrift,' an essay called "Religion without Metaphysics," of which the following are the principal points:--

"He starts with the observation that theologians of the new school have been turning more and more away from the metaphysical element of religion, and seeking to deduce the claims and the nature of religion from moral phenomena. Some of us, he says, have followed this road to its very end, and are now minded to detach religion from metaphysics altogether--to consider it to be not a view of the world, but a view of life, while we both describe and preach it as moral idealism. . . .

"Van Hamel, also, goes first of all to history, as our own countryman has done, to show that his religion is the true religion of history--the essence that remains when the accidental forms are stripped off. Religion, he maintains, has been everywhere and always essentially a view of life, and then a view of the world, to which the view of life, whatever it might be, gave rise. Every religion is a philosophy--a theory of the world; but this is not the most important element of it: the root of the matter has always been the view that was taken of life and its phenomena.

"Supernaturalism, in fact, is not religion. It becomes religion only when it is the expression of human needs. Only when the higher world is regarded in its relation to man's own need, whatever that may be, do those sentiments and dispositions arise which we call religion. Only when the man takes one or another of his ideals as the standard of the history and government of the world, so that it all subserves that ideal, and the gods work to realise it, does his philosophy become more than an idle imagination--does it become religion. And the main element in this religion is not the supernatural theory of the world--that is merely the formal side of it; the main thing is the peculiar conception of life--the peculiar direction of wishes and expectations; these are what confer on a religion its distinctive character. Thus, when the life is little more than material and sensuous, the gods will be mere natural phenomena. As society is developed, and the social instincts gain in power, the gods of the family of the tribe--of the race--appear. Jahveh is, first of all, the reflection of the national sentiment of Israel on its ideal side. As moral life is developed, moral gods appear, or those already in existence receive a more distinctly moral character. As life becomes more complex, this complexity is reproduced in the forms of religion, and we have polytheism. When one tendency becomes predominant, and other needs are thrown into the shade, religion grows monotheistic. Monotheism may also be the reflection of an impulse towards harmony--oneness in life.

"If this be a true account of the nature of religion, then Christianity may properly be called Moral Idealism. It is a religion in which neither sensuous life, nor national life, nor social life, nor ecclesiastical life, but purely moral life, is elevated to the ideal power, the highest element which is most worthy of God. Jesus is conscious of a power which carries Him irresistibly forward--is practically absolute--makes Him the champion of all right against all wrong--is ever close to Him, and fills Him with unspeakable happiness. He loves this power--calls it the Father in heaven. . . .

"As long as men are supernaturalists, they instinctively elevate their ideals to the throne of the universe. Imagination refuses nothing that sentiment requires. His god, man has no difficulty in supposing, rules heaven and earth in the interests of his requirements--his ideals. The true explanation of the universe is supplied by his life, or the fortune and future of his nation, or the coming of the kingdom of heaven of which he dreams. Thus, while supernaturalism prevails, the view of life which is the material of religion, is easily converted into a view of the world, with which religion is then identified.

"But take away supernaturalism, not only the older mechanical forms of it, but that notion of a Providence ruling all things in the interests of the good, that is, for the realisation of our ideals, which is as much a form of supernaturalism as the belief in miracles,--take away all idea of a purpose, an end, which things subserve; that is an unscientific notion. It is thought to be the very essence of Christianity--but this is not the case. Christianity is not a theory of the course of affairs at all. Let us acknowledge that nature goes her own way, and cares nothing for our wants, and would not be nature at all if she did otherwise.

"Then is religion abolished? By no means. You have still what is the essence of Christianity, though you have lost the form--the view of life, the attitude in the practical world, which Jesus introduced. We have still our moral ideals. These are the only sources from which religion springs, these alone give any religion at the stage in the world's history its substance and its authority.

"Here our author finds it necessary to define further what is meant by detaching religion from metaphysics, and calling it a view of life and not a view of the world. He does not deny the value of metaphysics in their own place; only he says they have nothing to do with religion, which is based on facts, experiences, and not on theories. When we call religion a view of life, we mean a way of taking life, a direction of the life, not a theory of life. It is a mode of grasping life practically. This can stand on its own feet--it has no need of theories, which, after all, are not the parents of religion but its children--which have been invented to account for a thing that existed before them, and can quite well continue to exist without them. Reasoning can do nothing to increase the reality and authority of the experiences from which religion springs; they are original, and suffice for themselves.

"And if it be asked, How do you know that your ideals on which alone you base your religion are true, are real things, and not merely your own subjective fancies, and if they do not need some support from without before you can place such implicit confidence in them? this leads into the question of the basis of morality, and we do not feel called upon to give a solution of it. We do not pretend that our ideals supply us with absolute truth, and for us at our present stage of culture they are absolute. They are to be judged simply by their practical power. They are not immovable--they come to us from the outside, and what we call the highest is for ever changing. What is the highest to-day may to-morrow have yielded to a higher. But the highest while it is with us has an indefeasible claim to our devotion, a claim which reasoning did not give and which reasoning cannot take away. This is not religion in the old sense, he frankly admits. If the essence of religion reside either in supernaturalism or in metaphysics, in the recognition of a real object of worship or in the transcendent character of the universe, then there is no religion here. . . . He asserts, however, that the essence of what has been hitherto called religion is here preserved."

Footnotes:
    204. Theologisch Tijdschrift, March 1875. Dr. I. Hooykaas, "Ter Beschrijving van de Ethische Richting."
    205. Theologisch Tijdschrift, September 1874. A. G. van Hamel, "Godsdienst zonder metafysica."

IV

(Lecture I., page 26.)

REVELATION AND THE DEVELOPMENT OF DOCTRINE.

It is only an untenable idea of Revelation that can be supposed at variance with the idea of the development of Christian Doctrine. If we identify Revelation with its record--in other words, with Scripture--then it might be assumed that Divine truth was something absolutely fixed ion the text of Scripture (although even in this case the truth would vary according to the different ways of interpreting it); but Revelation can only be rightly conceived as a new force of spiritual light and knowledge communicated to a spiritual intelligence. This force enters, like every other force of knowledge and morality, into the higher culture of the race, and, from a supernatural point of view, is the most powerful factor in advancing that culture. But it works organically like other elements of human progress. It is not a definite formula laid upon the human intelligence, but a definite impulse communicated to it.

The Hebrew race were chosen by God to be the recipients of this higher spiritual knowledge; and through the writings of the Hebrew prophets, who were the special organs of Revelation, the Divine truth communicated to them has been imparted to mankind in general. These writings contain the Revelation, or are the record of it. Their true purport is not to be gathered by a mere induction of texts or proof passages, but by a living and sympathetic insight into the true spirit and structure of their thoughts, and its organic relations with all the spiritual thought of succeeding ages. The interpreter, in short, must rise to the spiritual level of the prophets' mind (through the record which has been preserved of that mind), and so reach the heart of the Revelation communicated to it. It is only in this way that what was Revelation to the prophets can at the same time be Revelation to us-Revelation in every case

John Tulloch, D.D.

being, by its very terms, not a dead letter, but a living light in the mind and heart.

In this manner Revelation enters as a new and ever-renewing factor into human thought, continually enlarging, enlightening, and purifying it, and religious doctrine is the ever-fresh product of this process of spiritual education. It is the Divine truth originally communicated to the prophetic mind-- but which, just in virtue of its Divine originality, has continued to grow in the spiritual consciousness of humanity in connection with all the higher elements of that consciousness; and so from time to time has been moulded or translated into new forms of expression, adapted to new necessities, and in order to meet new forms of error. The idea of the development of Doctrine, therefore, instead of being opposed to the idea of Revelation, may be said to presuppose this latter idea, and to rest upon it. The difficulty of discriminating what is merely human, or as it is called "natural," in the product from what is divine or "supernatural," is an inherent difficulty which no theory of Revelation can extricate, and which is least of all got rid of by the theory which identifies Revelation with its record, or supposes doctrine to be a mere deduction from textual premises, or parts of the letter of Scripture brought together in supposed logical order,

V

(Lecture II., page 29.)

NATURE AND EVIL.

The most remarkable indictment of Nature as a source of evil rather than of good is to be found in Mr. J. S. Mill's posthumous Essays, recently published. The passage is one which must be held to show the weakness rather than the strength of the writer's mind. It is steeped throughout in that unconscious Anthropomorphism which is the professed bane of the modern school--and yet so often a distinctive note of their writings. Few men were more deeply tinged with this spirit than Mr. Mill--to the credit of his earnest and deeply philanthropic character; and yet while lavishing what can be called little else than abuse upon Nature, in the interests of man, apparently he refused to see in man himself anything but an outcome of the same cosmic Forces which he so vigorously denounced:--

"In sober truth, nearly all the things which men are hanged or imprisoned for doing to one another, are Nature's everyday performances. Killing, the most criminal act recognized by human laws, Nature does once to every being that lives; and in a large proportion of cases, after protracted torture such as only the greatest monsters whom we read of ever purposely inflicted on their living fellow-creatures. . . . Nature impales men, breaks them as if on the wheel, casts them to be devoured by wild beasts, burns them to death, crushes them with stones like the first Christian martyr, starves them with hunger, freezes them with cold, poisons them by the quick or slow venom of her exhalations, and has hundreds of other hideous deaths in reserve, such as the ingenious cruelty of a Nabis or a Domitian never surpassed. . . . She mows down those on whose existence hangs the wellbeing of a whole people, perhaps the prospects of the human race, for generations to come, with as little compunction as those whose death is a relief to themselves, or a blessing to those under their noxious influence. Such are Nature's dealings with life. Even when she does not intend to kill, she inflicts the same tortures in apparent wantonness. In the clumsy provision which she has made for that perpetual renewal of animal life, rendered necessary by the prompt termination she puts to it in every individual instance, no human being ever comes into the world but another human being is literally stretched on the rack for hours or days, not unfrequently issuing in death. Next to taking life (equal to it according to a high authority) is taking the means by which we live; and Nature does this too on the largest scale and with the most callous indifference. A single hurricane destroys the hopes of a season; a flight of locusts, or an inundation, desolates a district; a trifling chemical change in an edible root starves a million of people. The waves of the sea like banditti seize and appropriate the wealth of the rich, and the little all of the poor, with the same accompaniments of stripping, wounding, and killing, as their human antitypes. Everything, in short, which the worst men commit either against life or property, is perpetrated on a larger scale by natural agents. . . . Even 'the love of order,' which is thought to be a following of the ways of Nature, is in fact a contradiction of them. All which people are accustomed to deprecate as 'disorder,' and its consequences, is precisely a counterpart of Nature's ways. Anarchy and the Reign of Terror are overmatched in injustice, ruin, and death, by a hurricane and a pestilence."--'Three Essays on Religion,' p. 28 et seq.

The Christian Doctrine of Sin

VI

(Lecture II., page 32.)

COMPARATIVE THEOLOGY.

It will be apparent to all students of comparative theology how little I have ventured to touch the problems of this science, although I have been deeply interested in it for many years, in connection with my own special studies in the historic development of Christian Doctrine. My aim has been,--leaving aside all the difficult, and, as it appears to me, as yet insoluble questions, as to the chronology and external history of the great religions antecedent to Christianity,--to sketch from the general substance or contents of their thought the steps of advance on the special question of Evil--a comparatively easy task, for which there are abundant materials. The outward relations of the ancient Egyptian religion, or of the religions of Western Asia, to the oriental faiths--Vedism, Brahmanism, Zoroastrianism, Buddhism,--and again of these faiths to one another--especially the historical relations of Vedism and Zoroastrianism,--are subjects quite beyond my powers to meddle with. The view of the latter subject suggested in the text is that held by the most competent inquirers, whose moderation of judgment and good sense, as well as learning, excite the confidence of the second-hand student on such matters.

The following brief statements,--the first from Bunsen's God in History' (Miss Winkworth's translation, from which my quotations in the text are uniformly made), and the second quoted in Max Müller's Chips from a German Workshop,' from a well-known Sanscrit scholar,--speak for themselves:--

"The migration from Bactria to India took place, as we shall see, anterior to the reformation of the Bactrian faith by Zoroaster. The Vedic hymns themselves may be in part coeval with that reformation; but they are the hymns of the ancient faith, which in the original parent-land of the race was superseded, if not extirpated, by Zoroaster and their language is the most ancient monument of the Bactrian consciousness."--Bunsen,' God in History,' i. 274.

"Professor Roth, of Tubingen, has expressed the mutual relation of the Veda and Zend-Avesta under the following simile: The Veda,' he writes, and the Zend-Avesta, are two rivers flowing from one fountain-head: the stream of the Veda is the fuller and purer, and has remained truer to its original character; that of the Zend-Avesta, has been in various ways polluted, has altered its course, and cannot, with certainty, be traced back to its source.' "--Miller on the Zend-Avesta, Chips,' &c,, ii. 87.

VII

(Lecture II., page 33.)

SAVAGE NOTIONS OF EVIL.

The following illustrative passages are from Sir John Lubbock's well-known volume on the Origin of Civilisation and the Primitive Condition of Man' (3d ed.):--

"The Hottentots, according to Thunberg, have very vague ideas about a good Deity. They have much clearer notions about an evil spirit, whom they fear, believing him to be the occasion of sickness, death, thunder, and every calamity that befalls them.' The Bechuanas attribute all evil to an invisible god, whom they call Murimo, and never hesitate to show their indignation at any ill experienced, or any wish unaccomplished, by the most bitter curses.'"--P. 212.

"The Abipones of South America, so well described by Dobritzhoffer, had some vague notions of an evil spirit, but none of a good one. The Coroados of Brazil acknowledge no cause of good, or no God, but only an evil principle, which . . . leads him astray, vexes him, brings him into difficulty and danger, and even kills him.'"--P. 213.

"When Burton spoke to the Eastern negroes about the Deity, they eagerly asked where he was to be found, in order that they might kill him; for they said, Who but he lays waste our homes, and kills our wives and cattle?'"--P. 214.

VIII

(Lecture II., page 38.)

APOLLO.

These, amongst other attributes and characteristics of Apollo, are very clearly brought out in Mr Gladstone's admirable paper on "Homerology: I.--Apollo," in the Contemporary Review' for March 1876.

We quote a few sentences specially with reference to the Messianic functions attributed to Apollo in relation to Zeus:--

"1. He alone of the active gods is in entire and unvarying conformity with the will of Zeus, and is his messenger and agent for the most important purposes.

"2. He alone of male deities has the title Dios huios, son of Zeus.

"3. He alone of male deities is termed Aii philos, dear to Zeus, and is addressed by him as phile Phoibe.

"4. He alone shares with Zeus (Il. xiii. 154) the title of theon horistos.

"6. Apollo is the defender of Heaven against rebellion."

IX

(Lecture II., page 50.)

BRAHMA.

Referring to a passage which he quotes from the first book of the 'Sama-Veda,' Bunsen says:--

"Here we have the portentous word which divides the India of the Ganges from that of Indus, and in general the later religious consciousness of India from the Irano-Aryan. But we have by no means the noun masculine Brahma, the supreme god of the Brahmans, who are his priests. We have the neuter Brahma, an abstract noun, belonging entirely to the ideal world; which has its tangible roots in no historical tradition, but rather in a thoroughly externalistic treatment of the ancient Vedic sacrificial rites. According to Haug, it would appear from his researches into the Aryo-Zendic remains that the word Brahma originally signified the strewing of the sacrificial grass on the spot appointed for the immolation, or the contemplation of this holy work, from which it was extended to the contemplation of every holy act. Here we find the stepping-stone to the objective meaning according to which the neuter Brahma, as an abstract noun, denotes the Divine, the Godhead; philosophically therefore the Absolute, Unconditioned, Eternal, which is placed in opposition to the temporal, the phenomenal, the imperfect, and conditioned."--Bunsen's God in History,' i. 319.

X

(Lecture III., page 67.)

NARRATIVES OF THE CREATION AND OF THE FALL.

It is a well-known commonplace of modern criticism that the primary creation narrative (Gen. i-ii. 3,) and the narrative beginning with the fourth verse of the second chapter to the end of the third chapter, are from different sources.

"The book of Genesis was not written by one man, but was put together from works of very different dates; works, too, whose authors by no means all stood upon the same religious level. This very chapter will furnish us with illustrations of the fact, for immediately after the first account of the creation, a second follows, which by no means agrees with it. . . . The same writer" (who gives the second account of creation) "continues his narrative, and tells us how Paradise was lost."--The Bible for Young People, by Dutch Divines' (translation), i. 52, 58.

Of the question as to how these and other sections of Genesis are related to one another, Oehler says (Old Test. Theology, i. 74): "I certainly consider that the present shape of Genesis arose by the re-editing of an Elohistic narrative, and the interpolation of Jehovistic passages. But, at the same time, it must appear improbable that the author would place at the head of his work two contradictory accounts of the creation.

The Christian Doctrine of Sin

XI

(Lecture III., page 91.)

NATIONAL IMPORTANCE OF THE HEBREW PROPHETS.

"Their [the Jewish] religion, gave existence to an inestimably precious unorganised institution, the Order (if it may be so termed) of Prophets. Under the protection, generally though not always effectual, of their sacred character, the prophets were a power in the nation often more than a match for kings and priests, and kept up in that little corner of the earth the antagonism of influences which is the only real security for continued progress. Religion, consequently, was not there--what it has been in so many other places--a consecration of all that was once established, and a barrier against further improvement. The remark of a distinguished Hebrew, that the Prophets were in Church and State the equivalent of the modern liberty of the press, gives a just but not an adequate conception of the part fulfilled in national and universal history by this great element of Jewish life; by means of which, the canon of inspiration never being complete, the persons most eminent in genius and moral feeling could not only denounce and reprobate, with the direct authority of the Almighty, whatever appeared to them deserving of such treatment, but could give forth better and higher interpretations of the national religion, which thenceforth became part of the religion. Accordingly, whoever can divest himself of the habit of reading the Bible as if it was one book, which until lately was equally inveterate in Christians and in unbelievers, sees with admiration the vast interval between the morality and religion of the Pentateuch, or even of the historical books, and the morality and religion of the Prophecies,--a distance as wide as between these last and the Gospels. Conditions more favorable to progress could not easily exist; accordingly the Jews, instead of being stationary, like other Asiatics, were, next to the Greeks, the most progressive people of antiquity, and, jointly with them, have been the starting-point and main propelling agency of modern cultivation."--J. S. Mill's Representative Government,' p. 41.

XII

(Lecture III., page 96.)

HEBREW PROPHECY AND THE QUESTION OF EVIL.

The following is the passage from Kuenen's Religion of Israel' alluded to in the text. It appears to me expressed in far too general terms, and to ignore altogether some of the deepest elements of the prophetic teaching:--
"The older Israelitish prophets and prophetic historians had not hesitated to derive even evil, moral evil not excepted, from Jahveh: the belief that Jahveh directed all things was so strong in them, that they did not recoil from the consequence. Even the second Isaiah--perhaps with an eye to, but yet at variance with, the Persian dualism with which he was acquainted-had put these words into Jahveh's mouth:--

I form the light and create darkness,
I make peace and create evil;
I, Jahveh, do all these things.'

But it is not unnatural that objections to this conception should have arisen in the minds of some. Jahveh's moral purity seemed to them to be not uninjured by being thus made the immediate cause of sin. The remedy was at hand. Anro-Mainyus was not unknown to the Jews, and Satan stood ready as it were to undertake his part."--Kuenen's Religion of Israel' (translation), iii. 40.

XIII

(Lecture IV., page 109.)

THE ESSENES AND THE INFLUENCE OF DUALISTIC SPECULATION IN PALESTINE IN THE FIRST CENTURY.

The following abbreviated extracts from Dr. Lightfoot's recent essay on "The Colossian Heresy" bear out what is said in the text:--

"The Essene is the great enigma of Hebrew history. Admired alike by Jew, by Heathen, and by Christian, he remains a dim, vague outline. . . . And yet, by careful use of the existing materials, the portrait of this sect may be so far restored. . . . The Essene was exceptionally rigorous in his observance of the Mosaic ritual. . . . His respect for the law extended also to the lawgiver. After God, the name of Moses was held in the highest reverence. He who blasphemed his name was punished with death. In all these points the Essene was an exaggeration, almost a caricature, of the Pharisee. . . .

"To the legalism of the Pharisee, the Essene added an asceticism which was peculiarly his own, and which in many respects contradicted the tenets of the other sect. The honourable and even exaggerated estimate of marriage which was characteristic of the Jew, found no favour with the Essene. Marriage was to him an abomination. . . . But his ascetic tendencies did not stop here. The Pharisee was very careful to observe the distinction of meats lawful and unlawful, as laid down by the Mosaic code, and even rendered these ordinances vexatious by minute definitions of his own. But the Essene went far beyond him. He drank no wine, he did not touch animal food. . . . Again, in hot climates oil for anointing the body is almost a necessary of life. From this, too, the Essenes strictly abstained. . . .

"From these facts it seems clear that Essene abstinence was something more than the mere exaggeration of Pharisaic principles. The rigour of the Pharisee was based on his obligation of obedience to an absolute external law. The Essene introduced a new principle. He condemned in any form the gratification of the natural cravings, nor would he consent to regard it as moral or immoral only, according to the motive which suggested it or the consequences which flowed from it. It was in itself an absolute evil. He sought to disengage himself, as far as possible, from the conditions of physical life. In short, in the asceticism of the Essene we seem to see the germ of that Gnostic dualism which regards matter as the principle, or at least the abode, of evil. . . .

"An esoteric doctrine, relating to angelic beings, may have been another link which attached Essenism to the religion of Zoroaster. . . .

"This Jewish sect exhibits the same exclusiveness in the communication of its doctrines. Its theological speculations take the same direction, dwelling on the mysteries of creation, regarding matter as the abode of evil, and postulating certain intermediate spiritual agencies as necessary links of communication between heaven and earth. And lastly, its speculative opinions involve the same ethical conclusions, and lead in like manner to a rigid asceticism. If the notices relating to these points do not always explain themselves, yet read in the light of the heresies of the apostolic age and in that of subsequent Judæo-Gnostic Christianity, their bearing seems to be distinct enough; so that we should not be far wrong if we were to designate Essenism as Gnostic Judaism.

"The Essenes of whom historical notices are preserved were inhabitants of the Holy Land. Their monasteries were situated on the shores of the Dead Sea. We are told, indeed, that the sect was not confined to any one place, and that members of the order were found in great numbers in divers cities and villages."--Lightfoot on Colossians and Philemon, p. 82 et seq.

XIV

(Lecture IV, page 122.)

DR. J. MÜLLER ON LOVE TO GOD, AND SIN AS ITS OPPOSITE.

J. Müller, in his well-known elaborate treatise on 'The Christian Doctrine of Sin,' has worked out at length the idea of sin as selfishness, or the antithesis of love to God. I agree with those who think (Dr. Hodge, 'Syst. Theol.' ii. 149, and others) that Müller has made too much of this idea, in trying to reduce all forms of sin to selfishness as their essence; but I cannot mention this earnest and rich-minded theologian without expressing the obligation which I owe to the study of his great work on the subject of my Lectures. I am sensible that trains of thought derived from it long ago (when I made it a special study, and introduced it to the knowledge of many English readers, probably for the first time, in the 'British Quarterly Review,' Nov. 1851) still linger in my present exposition of the subject--different as my point of view now is. The reader may find some evidence of this in the following brief extracts:--

"Love is the inmost soul of all moral ordinances; and all deep reverence for law, all obedience to a higher will, all those sacred energies which hold human life together, and confine its activity within accurately-defined spheres, are only love in disguise; and, like the Old Testament law in the history of the human race, these when defined and embodied in the life of the individual are paidagogoi (Gal. iii. 24) for the kingdom of love revealed. Love can take root only in the soil of earnest strictness; true liberty can germinate only beneath the closely-enveloping sheath of self-limitation and submission to law.

"But love can only become the generative principle of a higher life when it makes itself manifest in its.. true character. It does not show itself in its fulness until it becomes conscious of God as its absolute object, and of all its other objects in their true relation to Him. Thus is the heavenly magnet found which is able, not for the passing moment of enthusiastic excitement only, but continually, to guide and sustain the life, of man over the dark mysterious sea in which the powers of the deep and the burden of its own sins and sorrows ever tend to sink it. . . .

"But sin is not only the absence of love to God; for with the negation of our true relation to Him there is the affirmation of a false one. Unbelief in the true God and the revelation of His holiness always involves a contrary belief, if it be only in the sufficiency of one's own critical and sceptical understanding. Upon the disappearance of the divine principle, there immediately ensues the entrance of a principle opposed to God, according to the saying of Christ, 'He who is not with me is against me.' Man cannot abandon his true relation to God without setting up an idol in God's stead. . . .

"The idol which man in sin sets up in the place of God can be none other than himself. He makes self and self-satisfaction the highest aim of his life. To self his efforts ultimately tend, however the modes and directions of sin may vary. The innermost essence of sin, the ruling and penetrating principle in all its forms, is selfishness.

"Man must be a personal being--an ego--if he be capable of holy love; and if he excludes holy love from his inner life, his natural self-love degenerates into selfishness, the disease of self, the corruption of self-love."--Müller's Christian Doctrine of Sin,' i. 115, 131, 134.

XV

(Lecture IV., page 132).

AUGUSTINE AND CALVIN ON HUMAN CORRUPTION.

The expressions in the text are to be found in the second book of Calvin's Institutio Christianæ Religionis:' the first, in the close of the second chapter of that book, being a quotation from Augustine (De Verbis Apost., Serm. 10)--"Nostrum nihil nisi peccatum;" and the second being the title of the third chapter of the same book. I am quite aware that both these modes of expression are capable of a strictly evangelical interpretation; or, in other words, that there is a sense in which they may be said to be in consistency with our Lord's teaching. And I am far from attributing to Calvin especially, a lack of balance and comprehensiveness of judgment in dealing with the question of sin. No one can read the two chapters to which I refer without seeing that this would be doing Calvin injustice (as, indeed, injustice is often done to his special views). In the very same chapters, for example, he freely allows a good side in human nature, or at least an undestroyed power of distinguishing good and evil ("ratio, qua discernit homo inter bonum et malum"--L. II. c. ii. § 13)--even a power of virtue ("ad virtutis studium facultas"), conspicuously illustrated in such men as Camillus (L. II. c. iii. § 4). Calvin is seldom deficient in comprehensiveness of intellectual judgment. But he is none the less narrow, and sometimes unfair in tone. Neither he nor Augustine can frankly admit that what is good in human nature is after all really good. Admitting, for example, the external virtue of such a natural man as Camillus, he yet asks, "What if his mind was depraved, which it must have been if he was only a natural man?" (ibid.) In other words, there is a back-lying theory of human depravity which colours, in both these theologians, all their estimates of human life and character. Dogmatic abstractions are constantly obtruding upon their line of thought, and giving a direction to it very different from the broad and fair representations of the Gospels, where everything stands for what it really is of good or of evil, without any distorting and confusing effects of abstract theory. The tone is different in the two cases. This is all that is meant by the observation in the text.

XVI

(Lecture V., page 140.)

ST. PAUL'S VIEW OF LAW.

Speaking of St. Paul's definition of the word "law," Reuss, in his History of Christian Theology in the Apostolic Age," says:--

"Primarily, this word signifies, purely and simply, the law of Moses as contained in the Pentateuch, or even a particular article of that law. "The Jews, however, had already in their common speech extended the circle of this notion, and designated by the term law the entire Old Testament, less in the literary sense--according to which the prophets were added, to complete the idea of the volume--than in the theological sense, all the other books being thus regarded as corollaries of the Mosaic legislation. It may be boldly affirmed that in most of the passages in which Paul makes use of the word law, it is in the historical or literary sense; the allusion is to the Old Testament as a whole, not to the Pentateuch in particular: on this account the term has most frequently that which was called in the old theology the economic signification--that is, it stands for the entire Old Testament economy."--P. 33, 34.

XVII

(Lecture V., page 155.)

CONFLICT OF THE FLESH AND MIND.

The following is part of Neander's exposition of this subject:--

"When the law in its glory, the moral archetype, first revealed itself to the higher nature of man, he was filled with earnest desire to seize the revealed ideal; but this desire only made him more painfully sensible of the chasm which separated him from the object after which he aspired. Thus, what appeared at first a blissful ideal, by the guilt of death-producing sin, became changed into its opposite. The higher nature of man aspiring after a freer self-consciousness, is sensible of the harmony between itself and the divine law, in which it delights; but there is another power, the power of the sinful principle striving against the higher nature, which, when a man is disposed to follow the inward divine leading, drags him away, so that he cannot accomplish the good by which alone his heavenly nature is attracted. In the consciousness of this wretched disunion, he exclaims, Who shall deliver me from this power of sin?' . . .

"By the opposition between the inner man and the law in the members or the flesh, Paul certainly does not mean simply the opposition between spirit and sense; for if the spirit were really so animated by the good which is represented in the law, as it ought to be, according to its original nature and destination, its volitions would be powerful enough to subordinate sense to itself. . . . He therefore intends by these terms to express the opposition between the depressed higher nature of man, and the sinful principle which controls the actions of men."--Neander's Hist. of the Planting and Training of the Christian Church,' Bohn's translation, p. 431, 432.

XVIII

(Lecture V, page 158.)

SIN.-CONSCIOUSNESS OF SIN.

The following are the statements referred to in the text:--

"The answer to this question," says Baur, "lies in the undeniable truth, that sin is what it is essentially and simply through man's consciousness of it; where there is no consciousness of sin, there is no sin."--Baur's 'St. Paul,' p. 141.

"In the apostle's language, consciousness is presupposed in the sin itself; not reflected on it from without. That which gives it the nature of sin is conscientia peccati. As Socrates, a little inverting the ordinary view and common language of mankind, declared all virtue to be knowledge; so the language of St. Paul implies all sin to be the knowledge of sin. Conscientia peccati peccatum ipsum est . . . If, from the apostle's ideal point of view, we regard the law, not as the tables given on Mount Sinai, or the books of Moses, but as the law written on the heart, the difficulty is, not how we are to identify the law

The Christian Doctrine of Sin

with the consciousness of sin, but how we are to distinguish them. . . . In the language of metaphysical philosophy, we say that the subject is identical with the object;' in the same way sin implies the law. The law written on the heart, when considered in reference to the subject, is simply the conscience. The conscience, in like manner, when conceived of objectively, as words written down in a book, as a rule of life which we are to obey, becomes the law. For the sake of clearness we may express the whole in a sort of formula. 'Sin = the consciousness of sin = the law.' From this last conclusion the apostle only stops short from the remembrance of the divine original of the law, and the sense that what made it evil to him was the fact that it was in its own nature good."--Jowett's Comm. on Epistle to Romans,' p. 504, 505.

XIX

(Lecture VI., page 179.)

DOCTRINE OF IMPUTATION OF SIN.

Mr. Jowett's remarks on this subject, to which we have alluded in the text, are deserving of quotation. There is force in what he says, and a much-needed caution, as to the tendency of theologians to generalise widely, and draw large propositions from a few Scriptural data--sometimes little more than "figures of speech." But, all the same, the line of thought concentrated in the two special passages to which he refers, and which form the basis of our Sixth Lecture, is essentially Pauline. The ideas involved in the passages, and the contrasts drawn in them betwixt Adam and Christ, enter into the heart of the apostle's thought, and cannot be explained away as mere rhetorical exaggeration.

"That so many opposite systems of Theology," he says, "seek their authority in Scripture, is a fair proof that Scripture is different from them all. That is to say, Scripture often contains in germ what is capable of being drawn to either side; it is indistinct where they are distinct; it presents two lights where they present only one; it speaks inwardly, while they clothe themselves in the forms of human knowledge. That indistinct, intermediate, inward point of view at which the truth exists but in germ, they have on both sides tended to extinguish and suppress. Passing allusions, figures of speech, rhetorical oppositions, have been made the foundation of doctrinal statements, which are like a part of the human mind itself, and seem as if they never could be uprooted, without uprooting the very sentiment of religion. Systems of this kind exercise a constraining power which makes it difficult for us to see anything in Scripture but themselves.

"For example, how slender is the foundation in the New Testament for the doctrine of Adam's sin being imputed to his posterity!--two passages in St. Paul at most, and these of uncertain interpretation. The little cloud, no bigger than a man's hand, has covered the heavens. To reduce such subjects to their proper proportions, we should consider: First, what space they occupy in Scripture; secondly, how far the language used respecting them is literal or- figurative; thirdly, whether they agree with the more general truths of Scripture and our moral sense, or are not rather repugnant thereto;' fourthly, whether their origin may not be prior to Christianity, or traceable in the after-history of the Church; fifthly, whether the words of Scripture may not be confused with logical inferences which are appended to them;. sixthly, in the case of this and some other doctrines, whether even poetry has not lent its aid to stamp them in our minds in a more definite and therefore different form from that in which the apostles taught them; lastly, how far in our own day they are anything more than words."--Jowett's Comm. on Epistle to Romans,' p. 180, 181.

##

(Lecture VI., page 185.)

AUGUSTINE'S TRANSLATION OF eph' ho (Rom. v. 12).--HIS VIEWS ON "ORIGINAL SIN."

Augustine's version of this phrase is found abundantly, as elsewhere, in his treatise De Peccatorum meritis et remissione,' which, he says (Retract. ii., 23), he was "compelled to write against the new heresy of Pelagius." Dealing with his own translation--in quo omnes peccaverunt--he applies the "quo" sometimes to "peccatum" and sometimes to Adam--"ille unus homo"--forgetful, apparently, as Migne points out in a note, that eph' o, could not agree with amartia--(Migne's ed., x. 115). All modern scholars may be said to unite in the statement of Baur that, "grammatically, eph' ho, cannot be taken in any other sense than because,'" or, as he expands the meaning, "the fact being that;" or again, Alford (in loc.), "on condition that."

John Tulloch, D.D.

"In the same treatise (L. III. c. iv.), Augustine discusses the question of original sin in relation to infants, and shows how plainly his whole views on this subject were dependent on his High Church or sacramentarian views as to the efficacy of baptism, and the consequent necessity of all infants being baptised in order to their salvation. His argument is as follows: Unless infants receive the benefit of the sacrament they are manifestly in danger of damnation. But damned they cannot be without sin. Now, since they have no sin of their own ("in vita propria"), it is necessary for us to credit them with original sin,--however unintelligible the mystery. It is enough to state this argument to show how entirely Augustine's tone of thought, on this as on many other matters, is removed from a modern or rational point of view. A fiction of sacramental efficacy is made the basis of an absurd argument. The name of Augustine, as I have said in the text, must always be held in respect; he possessed a profound spiritual nature and many noble qualities; but either as a writer or a thinker, there are few men who should be followed more cautiously. And never, certainly, should we allow the great apostle to speak to us only through his voice.

XXI

(Lecture VI., page 193.)

THEOLOGICAL MEANING OF GUILT.

I could have wished to collect an induction of passages in proof and illustration of the statement in the text, but it may be enough in the meantime to appeal to the following statements in confirmation of what I have said. Dr. Hodge's authority as a Calvinistic theologian will hardly be disputed.

"To impute sin, in Scriptural and theological language, is to impute the guilt of sin. And by guilt is meant not criminality, or moral ill-desert, or demerit, much less moral pollution, but the judicial obligation to satisfy justice. Hence the evil consequent on the imputation is not an arbitrary infliction, not merely a misfortune or calamity, not a chastisement in the proper sense of that word, but a punishment--i. e., an evil inflicted in execution of the penalty of law, and for the satisfaction of justice."--Hodge's 'Systematic Theology,' ii. 194.

"The venerable Assembly's Catechism, in answer to the question, Wherein consists the sinfulness of our estate by nature, says, In the guilt of Adam's sin,' &c. Now, as guilt is blameworthiness--desert of punishment; and as the compilers of that generally excellent compendium of faith cannot well be supposed to have intended to intimate that we are really blameable for an act performed by Adam,--they must have used the word in the general sense of legal liability, or obnoxiousness to punishment This is the sense in which it is used by all theologians in this country, and in America, except by the few who identify the race and its parent. To be guilty of Adam's sin is to be exposed by it to punishment--i. e., to the endurance of its consequences. Still the phrase is objectionable, since, though the endurance of its consequences was punishment to Adam, it Is not so to us. The constitution established with him was such as to expose us to the results of his conduct; but that exposure, or liability, is not guilt in any proper sense of the term, or in common parlance even, nor should it ever be so called. The child of a profligate parent is liable to disease, but he is never thought of as guilty. The term guilt always supposes personal transgression, except in technical theology, from which we would banish it."--Payne's Lectures on Original Sin,' p. 79, 80, note.

www.ingramcontent.com/pod-product-compliance
Lightning Source LLC
Chambersburg PA
CBHW032050090426
42744CB00004B/158